MEETINGS *That* MATTER

REVISED EDITION

Effective Meeting Management for Student Activities

Written and Compiled by
Earl Reum, Lyn Fiscus, Jeff Sherrill, and David Cordts

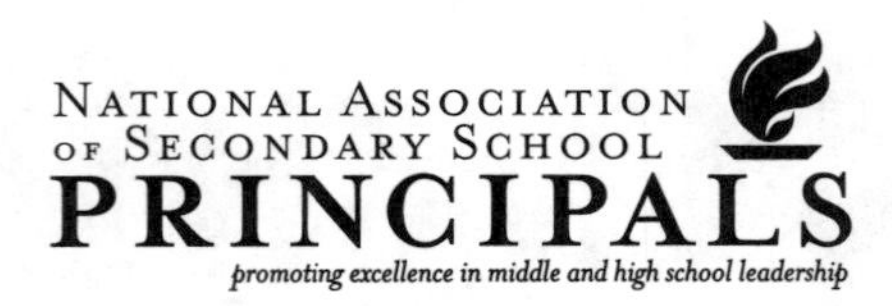

ABOUT THE AUTHORS

Earl Reum, a leadership education consultant and motivational speaker, addresses more than 100,000 students and advisers each year and has been a teacher, adviser, mentor, and advocate for student activities for more than 40 years.

Lyn Fiscus, editor of *Leadership for Student Activities* magazine since 1995, has written extensively on student activities topics and is a frequent presenter at student activities conferences.

Jeff Sherrill is the associate director for the National Association of Student Councils and middle level activity services at NASSP.

David Cordts is the associate director for the National Honor Society and National Junior Honor Society at NASSP.

1904 Association Dr. Reston, Va. 20191-1537
703-860-0200

ISBN: 0-88210-373-3

Product Number: 6200701

Foreword to the 1993 Edition

BY EARL REUM

Experts estimate that in the United States more than 11 million meetings take place each day. While many of these meetings are undertaken in an efficient and effective manner, others are often viewed simply as a waste of time. The hope of student activities meetings is that they will be good enough to involve, inspire, recognize, and plan for student life. Student leaders should take meetings seriously. When they learn the skills needed to run good meetings and understand the purposes of their organization and their roles within it, they can develop a great vision, which in turn creates great meetings.

My goals for our meeting include:

1. I want you to realize there are an enormous number of meetings held in the world on a daily basis—and most of them are ineffective because of a lack of goals, planning, commitment, or understanding.
2. I want you to learn meeting skills such as parliamentary procedure, interaction techniques, action planning, brainstorming, discussion groups, and other skills. The point is that each skill has a specific use in a meeting. We need to know which procedure to use in which meeting situation. We need to develop strategies for handling problems in meetings.
3. Meetings need to be planned around goals, participants, the facility, resources, and predictable outcomes. We need to analyze why, where, when, who, what, and how, then plan for a group to come to its decisions, its fulfillment, and its destiny because of the meeting.
4. We have responsibilities for making each meeting effective by planning it, participating in it ourselves, nurturing the participation of others, and then following up on what happened during the meeting.
5. We need to consider success in large group meetings and in small group sessions. We need to develop agendas for every kind of meeting, including the informal ones mentioned above.

Use this book to help make your meetings meaningful and magical!

Goals for the Revised Edition

■

In 2002, the board of directors of the National Association of Secondary School Principals (NASSP) adopted a position statement regarding student activities. In it, they included the following remarks:

> Beyond the standard curriculum of required and elective courses, schools enhance student learning and development by offering a range of cocurricular student activities. Student activities are integral to an education, providing opportunities for all students that support and extend academic learning. Student activities support the goal of teaching students to be responsible and fulfilled human beings, providing them with opportunities that develop character, critical thinking, sociability, and specific skills. (See Chapter 7 for the full text of the position statement.)

Meeting management is one of these essential skills that educators can help students develop through the students' participation in cocurricular activities. This revised text is designed to help activities advisers teach their student leaders to make the most of all of their meetings, big and small, formal and informal.

In developing this monograph, we drew primarily from three resources. We included the core of the 1993 edition, but reorganized and reformatted the text to enhance the value of the content. We also selected content from the curriculum guide for the National Student Leadership Camps previously sponsored by NASSP. Finally, we incorporated a variety of articles and resources from *Leadership for Student Activities* magazine, the official student activities publication from NASSP. These texts offer important additional commentary on the essential topic of meeting management.

This revised edition is a guide, both practical and theoretical. Skills exercises and worksheets are incorporated into every chapter along with notes and observations that provide background and support for those who work with students. We hope this edition will become an essential part of your student activities professional library.

—The Authors

CONTENTS

Why Meetings?

Through the years, the critics of meetings have spoken:

Meetings are indispensable when you don't want to do anything.
—John Kenneth Galbraith, economist

If you had to identify, in one word, the reason why the human race has not achieved, and never will achieve, its full potential, that word would be "meetings."
—Dave Barry, humorist

Meetings are a symptom of bad organization. The fewer the meetings the better.
—Peter Drucker, management theorist

A meeting is an event at which the minutes are kept and the hours are lost.
—Unknown

Despite these criticisms—some serious and some tongue in cheek—well-planned meetings are a key to an organization's effectiveness. It is through meetings that the organization establishes its identity, formulates policies, makes decisions, and discusses ideas. We are all members of communities and groups that conduct meetings. By participating in and learning to manage meetings, students develop:

- Personal life skills, talents, and abilities, including skills in organization, communication, leadership, problem solving, and interpersonal relations
- Knowledge and improved intellectual capabilities
- Social skills
- Loyalty, spirit, pride, and patriotic attitudes
- Willingness to serve the school and the community.

GENERAL PRINCIPLES

Good meetings don't just happen. To make meetings effective, you need to learn meeting management skills. The best way to do that is to start with these general guidelines, which help you better understand the group that is meeting.

1. Be familiar with the constitution and bylaws and the general structure of the group's activities.
2. Review the purposes, goals, and objectives of the organization and the kinds of activities that may help accomplish them.
3. Be familiar with school policies and administrative guidelines regarding student activities.
4. Understand the relationship of the organization to other organizations inside and outside of school.
5. Have a basic handbook for all members of the organization that includes the constitution and bylaws; organizational structure; purposes, goals, and objectives; school policies and guidelines related to the organization; and job descriptions. Members can add agendas, minutes, and other relevant information throughout the year.

MEETING PURPOSES

What purposes can meetings fulfill on campus? What are the most useful techniques that best carry out the goals of each meeting effectively?

Purpose	Techniques
To Inform: To communicate information	Movies, slides, lectures, panels, charts, visuals, overheads
To Persuade: To move members to understand and accept decisions	Lectures, charts, interaction, music, emotional appeal
To Explore Topics: To gather facts or opinions from the group	Brainstorm, buzz groups, quiz, group discussion, interaction, group participation
To Generate Ideas: To list group suggestions	Brainstorm, discussion groups, butcher paper listings
To Solve Problems: To define a problem and let the group solve it	Define, delineate the problem, propose, choose, use solutions
To Inspire: To celebrate and recognize accomplishments and motivate others to action	Music, focus, videos
To Make a Decision: To solve problems	Parliamentary procedure, consensus techniques
To Plan for the Group: To plan activities	Brainstorm, butcher paper listings, organizational worksheets
To Organize a Project/Event: To develop and implement plans	Organizational worksheets, planning guides, evaluations from previous events
To Recognize Outstanding Effort: To celebrate success and honor efforts	Music, refreshments, celebration

Keys for Successful Meeting Management: Conduct an annual training workshop for your organization's leaders where these elements are reviewed, renewed, and, if necessary, revised.

Effective Meetings

By Shannon Bloomstran

I taught high school history for 10 years. Any of my former colleagues will tell you that as much as I liked teaching, I hated meetings. We had department meetings, faculty meetings, committee meetings, and district curriculum meetings, just to name a few. On top of that, I sponsored the student council and that generated even more meetings. I never could put my finger on what it was that bugged me most about these meetings. Was it the administrator who stood up and said, "Okay, they told me I had to have something to talk about at these meetings. How are the bells working for you all?" Or maybe it was the counselor who said, "I know I put this memo in your mailboxes last week, but let me read it to you anyway." Grrrrrr. It sets my teeth on edge just to think about them.

In retrospect, the meetings, while usually necessary, were often poorly planned and poorly facilitated. I suppose I probably didn't dislike the meetings so much as the way they were run. The devil definitely is in the details. Because secondary teachers essentially run six meetings a day, I don't think we have a high tolerance for ineffectiveness. What's that adage about doctors making the worst patients? That's why many activity advisers have a tendency to jump in and run the meetings themselves rather than observe yet another pointless and fruitless gathering. However, it is easy and painless to teach your officers how to conduct meetings more effectively.

Determine the Purpose

It would be easy to solve everyone's meeting woes if all meetings were exactly alike. But activity groups meet for a number of different reasons, so make sure you look at each meeting as if it were its own unique entity. Is it educational in nature? At an educational meeting, you might hear committee updates or listen to the principal's ideas on a new attendance policy. Meetings can be social also, especially at the beginning of the year with all those new members. Many meeting hours are devoted to planning and decision making, while others are purely for evaluation. Still others may be for recognition or conflict resolution. Determining the purpose of the meeting helps solve many other organizational details--your student leaders just might discover they can't come up with a purpose and in that case, the meeting's canceled!

Set the Goals

After you've determined the purpose of the meeting, have your officers set some goals. Many groups set goals for the year, but how many set goals for individual meetings? Really hold your student leaders' feet to the fire and force them to be specific. Encourage goals like "Select the Homecoming theme and assign committees" rather than "plan for Homecoming." This way, fewer tasks will slip through the cracks and your members will feel a sense of accomplishment at the end of the meeting.

Ask them to fill in the blank, "By the end of the meeting we should have _____." Phrasing it this way keeps the focus on the product of the meeting as well as the process. It also makes setting the agenda relatively easy. Once your officers or other facilitators become adept at planning, they might not need your input in this step, but at least initially, you should supervise the goal-setting process.

Get Organized

To have a successful meeting, you need to do some preparation. Many meetings are doomed before they even start due to poor logistics. The room's too hot, no one can hear, or the speaker is late—any one of these can keep your meeting from being successful. Try to solve these problems before they emerge. Go back and review your purpose and goals. Keep those in mind when you consider things like how the room should be arranged and even where the meeting should be held. More informal meetings call for a relaxed setting, possibly with the chairs in a circle or at tables pushed together. For more formal meetings where important discussion needs to take place, chairs might be in rows. Perhaps you need an auditorium or lecture hall. Just make sure the setting matches the purpose.

Many groups like to offer snacks to meeting participants. Consider setting up a refreshment schedule at the start of the year. A principal I once worked for taught me that people are more likely to go along with your ideas if you offer them food. Who wants to argue on a full stomach?

Another facet of organization is publicity. Get the word out about the meeting time and place. Even if your group meets at the same time every week, it can't hurt to put up some signs or launch a phone tree.

Set the Agenda

It is especially important to consider your purpose when you set your agenda. Many groups follow a modified version of the order of business suggested by *Robert's Rules of Order*. They hear the minutes of the previous meeting, then hear committee reports, then old or unfinished business, then new business. This is a terrific template, but make sure that it suits your purpose.

Whatever format you use, it is wise to write down the agenda ahead of time. Be reasonable about what you can accomplish during one meeting. My dad, president of a bank, always said, "No meeting should last more than an hour; if it does, you should have scheduled two meetings." If your meetings continually get bogged down, try posting time limits right on the agenda. This will help to keep you on track. Also note on the agenda who will be speaking so no one will be caught off-guard. For example: "Decoration Committee Update—Jordan—3:00–3:10."

In planning your agenda, you can also determine any supplies you will need and who is responsible for them. Determine if you need things like audiovisual equipment, art supplies, or paper. Nametags are often helpful, especially at the beginning of the year.

Post the agenda in a conspicuous, predetermined location or hand copies out to participants ahead of time. Make sure your facilitator is familiar with the agenda well before the meeting starts.

If you can do nothing else, convince your officers to stick to the agenda—assuming of course it's well-planned. The only thing worse than a long meeting is a long, unproductive meeting. In most cases, an unproductive meeting can be avoided by simply sticking to the agenda. That said, a good facilitator should know the group well enough to know when it might be productive to deviate slightly. He or she should be able to sense fatigue or potential conflicts and be able to keep the group moving along.

To lessen conflict and increase camaraderie, some groups conduct a short icebreaker at the start of the meeting. Here are some easy ideas:

- Have students partner up and interview each other to learn "Five Fast Facts." Have the partners share.
- Post a quotation on the board when members arrive. Ask students to guess who said the quote.
- Pass out brainteasers for members to work on as everyone gets settled. Offer a small prize for whoever figures it out first.
- Some groups ask a different member to be responsible for each meeting's icebreaker. Remember to keep the icebreakers short and simple—you don't want to get bogged down before you even start.

Good Facilitation

Ideally, every meeting would be filled with excited participants just bursting to share their well-reasoned and insightful opinions. The real world, as most advisers know, often presents a far different picture. That's where a good facilitator comes in, and good facilitators are made, not born. Set up sessions at the beginning of the year to teach your officers some facilitation skills.

Right off the bat, they should know a good meeting requires input from its participants and a good facilitator has the ability to get input in a variety of different ways. Don't limit yourselves to asking participants to raise their hands in response to a question. That may work for some people and in some settings, but it shouldn't be a one-size-fits-all technique. Have students write down responses or work in small groups to discuss or propose ideas. Both ways help get input from students who may be too shy or intimidated to speak in front of a large group.

A good facilitator keeps her finger on the pulse of the group. One way to check the group's feeling is to use a game called Gunny Sacking. Pass out small slips of paper and ask participants to fill in the blank in this statement; "Right now I feel ___." Have them toss their responses in a hat and then have each one pull out someone else's response. Quickly go around the room, having participants read aloud one another's responses. If you hear responses like "bored," "tired," or "frustrated," you'll know it's time to redirect quickly.

You can ward off mounting frustration and fatigue by scheduling short breaks. Set a time limit, however, and stick to it. Try to minimize disruptions; your officers should have a plan of how to deal with disruptions before they happen. No one is advocating instituting a dictatorial regime, but for anything to get accomplished, you need as few disruptions as possible. Encourage your leaders to stimulate discussion and don't let the same few upperclassmen dominate. Try to get your freshmen involved as well. Urge them to stick to concrete issues. Ban phrases like "I heard that someone said..." Encourage them to comment on what they know for sure, no rumors or hearsay.

Wrapping Up the Meeting

Every good performer knows how to end the show on a high note. They don't drone on and on until the audience is half asleep, they always leave the audience wanting a little bit more. Ending a meeting is essentially no different. Make sure your facilitators know how to the end the meeting so everyone can leave feeling their valuable time was used productively. The facilitator should prepare a conclusion plan before the meeting, especially if you anticipate a conflict-ridden meeting.

Before adjourning, review any decisions you made, even the most basic ones. "So we decided our Homecoming theme will be Back in Black and the main colors will be black and silver." This accomplishes two goals: It gives everyone one more chance to hear the information and it reminds them that something important did take place. Your conclusion plan should also include a big thanks to participants. Some groups give out Kudos candy bars at the end to anyone who has been particularly helpful. Always announce your next meeting time and date and ask that participants write this information down.

Evaluation

Just as it is in the activity planning process, evaluation is an important part of the meeting planning process. For the first few meetings of the year, consider having a short debriefing session with your officers or facilitators after the meeting. Ask them how the meeting went and offer your observations. Help them process any conflict or disagreement so they don't leave angry or frustrated. Evaluation doesn't have to occur after every meeting, but try to conduct a meeting evaluation at least two or three times a semester. Include your members as well as your facilitators and you'll get a better sense of how you are doing. Always keep yourselves open to new ideas. Poll the members for their ideas as to how to improve meetings. Having members participate in the evaluation process helps avoid those "parking lot meetings," you know, the ones where everyone meets in the parking lot after the real meeting adjourns to discuss who said what about whom. They can really be destructive to morale and process.

If you think about it, in the real world many people spend much of their lives in meetings. Teaching your students effective facilitation skills can help them not only in their high school careers, but just might give them a leg up in the future job market.

Shannon Bloomstran is a former student council adviser and leadership teacher who is currently a freelance writer based in St. Louis, MO.

Types of Meetings

"An organization's results are determined through webs of human commitments born in webs of human conversations."

—Fernando Flores, philosopher, former Chilean minister of finance

A meeting happens any time two or more people get together to gather or give information, to express ideas, to persuade others, to plan action, to solve problems, to make decisions...whenever people gather to simply understand themselves and the world better.

To guarantee a fantastic meeting, leaders need to be certain that people are prepared to participate, that the discussion is interesting, that people feel comfortable, and that the group can work efficiently in the time available. Then, once a group determines a meeting is necessary, members must decide on the meeting process—the type of meeting that will help the organization reach its goals.

MEETING PROCESSES

Leaders can use many techniques to conduct a meeting. The goals of a meeting will determine the best meeting processes to use. Here are a number of meeting processes to consider:

Brainstorming. Group members contribute as many ideas as possible about a problem, a program, or a procedure, in a short amount of time. These ideas are considered at length after the brainstorming ends.

Parliamentary procedure. Groups use this tool to establish organization structure, define rules for conducting business, and codify decisions.

Action planning. This informal strategy helps groups make plans to achieve goals, often through consensus rather than formal voting. Group ownership is a hallmark of this technique, which calls for the participation of all members.

Interaction method. A facilitator and recorder post the group agenda, set ground rules, and guide interaction and participation. This technique promotes total participation, commitment, consensus, and ownership.

Group discussion. Small groups consider all sides of an issue. Later, the small groups reassemble to share ideas, resources, understandings, and solutions. This is an excellent technique for gathering input from all members of a large group.

BRAINSTORMING

Brainstorming is a way to stimulate creative thinking. Simply stated, it is the free expression of ideas on a given subject without evaluation by the group. Organizations of all types and sizes use brainstorming to solve business and management problems. Brainstorming is a useful method for developing ideas, encouraging participation, solving problems, and exploring possible courses of action in all sorts of meetings.

The essential elements of a brainstorming session follow:

1. The group leader writes the problem to be considered on a chalkboard or butcher paper. The leader states the question briefly, clearly, and in a manner that will stimulate thought and conversation.
2. The leader clarifies the reason the question is being posed by providing background information as well as information about how the ideas will be used.
3. The leader outlines the ground rules for brainstorming:
   a. Every idea is acceptable.
   b. Evaluation of the ideas is not allowed during the brainstorming. This includes both verbal evaluation and nonverbal expressions.
   c. The quantity of ideas is the goal; quality ideas will follow. (This is called freewheeling.)
   d. Hitchhiking—building on the contributions of others—is encouraged. Some of the best suggestions are stimulated by other people's ideas.
   e. There is a time limit.
4. People begin offering their ideas. The presenter lists each idea as quickly as possible and writes each exactly as given. Hesitation in recording an idea may be interpreted as disapproval. Usually the session begins with an initial spurt of ideas and then slows down. As the group members consider the ideas listed for a few minutes, they may come up with a new flurry of ideas. Writing down their own ideas can help them get their thoughts down.
5. After all ideas are recorded, the group discusses the suggestions together or divides into subgroups. Before breaking into subgroups, the members as a whole should identify the most promising ideas. Then, each subgroup selects 5–10 of the most promising suggestions to discuss. The subgroups report their results to the reassembled group. The entire membership tries to arrive at a group consensus regarding what ideas to implement and how.

A BRAINSTORMING EXERCISE

The facilitator may wish to do this sample exercise as a warm up prior to a real problem-solving brainstorming session.

Get Ready

The facilitator asks the participants to form small groups of approximately six members per group. Each group of six forms a circle and selects a secretary.

The facilitator provides a felt-tip marker and newsprint to each secretary and asks him or her to record every idea generated.

Get Set

When the groups are ready to begin, the facilitator explains the ground rules as follows: There will

TEN STEPS TO SUCCESSFUL BRAINSTORMING

1. Assemble participants. Ensure participants have varied backgrounds. Limit the number of participants to between 10 and 20.
2. Limit the scope of the problem you are solving. State the problem clearly and agree about the definition of all words used. Make sure everyone understands the stated proposition. A problem well-stated is a problem half-solved.
3. Create a noncritical atmosphere. No one is to do or say anything negative. No one, by look or action, may indicate that he or she thinks another's idea is silly or useless. The sky is the limit. Preposterous, screwball, and even impossible solutions are welcomed. An idea that seems weird may spark subsequent valuable contributions.
4. Record every contribution. Use one or two persons to record ideas.
5. Strive to elicit a lot of ideas rapidly. See how many good ideas you can get in five minutes or another specific amount of time.
6. Urge participants to improve on ideas, combine ideas, and add to other's ideas (hitchhiking).
7. Maintain control of participants. The chairperson must remain in control of the group. All group members must follow agreed upon procedures for introducing ideas. Keep track of the time.
8. Use questions to stimulate thinking. If the group gets bogged down, the chairperson may restate the problem or ask questions.
9. Decide on the merits of ideas. This is an essential step that the core group or an entirely different group of people should do promptly after brainstorming. The group will eliminate some ideas quickly and analyze and discuss others at length.
10. Select the best idea or method for solving the problem.

be no criticism during the brainstorming phase; far-out ideas are encouraged as they may trigger other, more practical, ideas for someone else; and the more ideas the better.

Go

Phase One: Generating. The facilitator announces the problem to be solved or the topic of the session. Each group is given five minutes (or other reasonable time to cover the problem) to share ideas using the ground rules as outlined.

Phase Two: Evaluating. When the generating phase is completed, the facilitator notifies the groups that the ban on criticism is over and asks them to evaluate their ideas and form a single list.

Phase Three: Regrouping. If there are four or more groups, the facilitator asks two groups to share ideas and form a single list.

Phase Four: Sharing. The facilitator asks participants to return to one large group. Secretaries act as spokespeople and take turns sharing their ideas. Participants are asked to pyramid or combine two or more ideas that might be used together.

Phase Five: Ranking. The facilitator writes the final list of ideas on the chalkboard and the group is asked to put them in rank order.

PARLIAMENTARY PROCEDURE

One common goal of meetings is to make decisions. The best procedure for making decisions as a group is parliamentary procedure, a system of rules and customs that many groups use to make decisions, conduct business, and secure action on proposals. *Robert's Rules of Order* is considered the authority on parliamentary procedure and is available at most bookstores and online.

Advantages of parliamentary procedure are:

1. Justice and courtesy are extended to each person.
2. Only one item of business is considered at a time.
3. The majority opinion is maintained.
4. The rights of the minority are respected.
5. It provides a standardized language for conducting business.

Disadvantages of parliamentary procedure are:

1. It may become so complicated that it obstructs, restrains, or hinders group discussion or action.
2. It is not universally understood.
3. It may not be the best technique for securing ideas and suggestions with regard to the problems involved.
4. It does not encourage creativity.

PARLIAMENTARY PROCEDURE: HOW IT WORKS

According to the National Association of Parliamentarians, "Fundamentally, parliamentary procedure defines how groups of people, no matter how formal or informal, can most effectively meet and make decisions in a fair, consistent manner—and make good use of everyone's time. Even a basic background in parliamentary principles can help you and your organization hold more efficient meetings." (www.parliamentarians.org).

The basic principles of parliamentary procedure are:

- Process is based on common sense and logic.
- All members have equal rights and privileges.
- Every person is entitled to have a voice, to understand, and to participate.
- The group makes decisions by voting.
- Only one issue is handled at a time.
- The meaning of each issue must be clear to every person before the vote is taken. When there is no further discussion, the group votes.
- Duties and powers may be delegated to individuals and subgroups of the whole, but the group maintains the right to make the final decision.
- It is the responsibility of the presiding officer to be fair and just.

ESSENTIALS OF PARLIAMENTARY PROCEDURE

- Parliamentary procedure helps groups make decisions through a formal structure.
- All decisions are reached through "motions," formal statements given to the group for consideration, discussion, and voting.
- Any member may "make a motion." It must be "seconded" to show that at least two people are interested in the idea.
- The presiding officer then "states the question," i.e., repeats the motion in brief, clear language.
- Members who wish to discuss the motion ask for "recognition by the chair." They discuss the facts of the proposal, not the personalities and motives of the proposers. No person who has spoken may speak again until everyone who wishes has had a turn.
- When there are no further questions or statements, the chairperson calls for a vote.
- The presiding officer does not vote except in the case of a tie.

MEETINGS IN MOTION

A key element of parliamentary procedure is handling motions fairly.

I. The Main Motion

A. Definition: The main motion is the major proposal or suggestion for action. It is the only way to bring business before the group.

B. Example:

Member: Rises, remains standing, waits for recognition, and addresses the chairperson: "Mr. President..." or "Madam Chairperson..."

Chairperson: Recognizes the member: "The chair recognizes (member's name if known)."

Member: Makes the motion: "I motion that..."

Member 2: Seconds the motion: "I second the motion." Seconding member need not address the chair, be recognized, or rise.

Chair: States the motion. "It is moved and seconded that....Is there any discussion?" Members wishing to speak for or against the motion must rise, address the chair, and are recognized. Members generally speak only once and limit their remarks to pertinent comments. When there seems to be a lull in the discussion the chair may ask, "Are you ready for the question?" or "Is there any further discussion?" If no one objects, the chair puts the motion to a vote.

Chair: The chair again repeats the motion: "It has been moved and seconded that....All in favor of the motion say 'Aye.' All those opposed say 'No.'" The chair then announces the results: "The motion is carried," or "The motion is lost." If the chair is not sure of the vote, he may ask for a show of hands or a standing vote. On some important matters there may be a need for a roll call vote.

C. Summary: Any member may make a motion after securing the floor and being recognized by the chair. A motion is out of order if other business is on the floor. A second is needed for the motion to be considered. The motion can be debated and amended and needs a majority vote to carry.

II. Subsidiary Motions

A. Definition: The subsidiary motions in some way alter or change the disposition of the main motion. They are always acted upon before the main motion.

B. Rank order: Each subsidiary motion may be acted upon in the order listed below. The further down the list, the higher the priority.

1. Postpone indefinitely: "I move the matter be postponed indefinitely." A second is required. The motion is debatable and is not amendable. A majority vote is needed. It is not amendable. This motion gives the opponents of a motion an opportunity to test their strength without risking a vote on the main motion. If they carry the motion, they can, in effect, kill the motion. If they lose, they still have a chance on the main motion.
2. Amend motion: "I move to amend the motion by striking the word(s)...and inserting the word(s)...." A motion may be amended by deleting and/or adding to the main motion. The amendment cannot be contrary to the spirit of the original motion. A second is required. The motion is debatable and can be amended. A majority vote is needed.
3. Substitute motion: "I move the following substitute motion: (the substitute motion)." A substitute motion ranks as an amendment to the main motion. Its purpose is to strike out the entire motion and insert in its place a more satisfactory motion. The procedure is the same as for an amendment.
4. Amend amendment: In general, this is the same procedure as for an amendment to the main motion, however it is not amendable. It pertains only to the original amendment and cannot refer to any part of the main motion not included in the original amendment. There can only be one amendment to each amendment.
5. Motion to refer: "I move that this matter be referred to the (name of the committee)." Generally the motion to refer is made to a committee. A second is required. It is debatable and amendable and requires a majority vote.
6. Postpone to set time: "I move that we postpone consideration of this motion until (time)." A second is required. It is debatable and amendable and requires a majority vote.
7. Previous question: "I move that we limit debate on this question to (time)." The purpose of this motion is to define the number and time of speeches or speakers. A second is needed; it is not debatable, but may be amended, and requires a two-thirds vote.
8. Table: "I move that we postpone consideration of this motion until (time)" or "I move the question be laid on the table." The purpose of this motion is to dispose of troublesome questions that will need long debate in order to deal with more important matters. A second is required. It is not debatable or amendable. It requires a majority vote.

III. Privileged Motions

A. Definition: Privileged motions are of such importance or urgency that they outrank all other motions.

B. Rank order: The following rank order is suggested. The further down the list, the higher the priority. They are all undebatable.

1. Orders of the day: The purpose of this motion is to bring the group back to the agenda or planned program. "Mr. Chairman, I call for the order(s) of the day" or "I move the consideration of the item on the agenda, namely (state)." A second is not required. It is not debatable or amendable. A majority vote is needed.

2. Questions of privilege: This relates to the personal rights, privileges, and comfort of the members. A member may interrupt a speaker. She stands and says, "I rise to a question of privilege (states question)." The chairman generally decides whether to proceed as requested or to declare suggestions out of order. It is not debatable, amendable, or voted upon. Business must continue after the matter is taken care of.
3. Recess: The purpose of a recess is to hold an intermission for meals, counting ballots, and the like. If a motion to recess is carried and seconded, the recess begins immediately. The motion is not debatable but is amendable as to the length of time to recess. A majority vote is needed.
4. Adjourn: The purpose of a motion to adjourn is to adjourn until a fixed time or until the next regular or special meeting. "I move we adjourn until (date, time, and place)" or "I move we adjourn." A second is required. It is not debatable and is amendable only as to date, time, and place. A majority vote is needed.

IV. Incidental Motions

A. Definition: Incidental motions concern matters of procedure arising out of business and must be settled at once.

B. Examples:

1. Point of order: Raised when there has been an alleged breach of parliamentary rules, the constitution, bylaws, and so on. A point of order can be made at any time; the member may interrupt the speaker. The point of order is usually resolved by the chair without discussion.
2. Appeal from decision of the chair: Used when a member believes the chairman made a wrong decision. The appeal must be made immediately after the decision and settled by vote. "I appeal from the decision of the chair (state appeal)." This motion requires a second, is debatable, and needs a majority vote. It is not amendable.
3. Suspend the rules: An agreement to temporarily waive rules of order for a specific reason. "I move to suspend the rules in order to...." A second is required. It is not debatable or amendable and requires a two-thirds vote.
4. Object: Used to avoid consideration of an embarrassing, irrelevant, or contentious motion. Must be made before any debate. "I object to the consideration of this motion." It is permissible to interrupt the speaker. A second is not required. It is not debatable, and a two-thirds vote is needed.
5. Division of the house: A standing vote is used to verify a vote that was just taken by voice or hand. The speaker rises and says, "I call for a division of the house." The chair decides and proceeds. If the use of the motion is abused, the chair may declare the speaker out of order. A second is not required; it is not amendable or debatable.
6. Parliamentary inquiry or information: A request for information. "I rise to ask a question (states question)." The chair may refer the question to the parliamentarian or answer it himself.
7. Permission to withdraw motion: A request that a motion be withdrawn must be made by the person making the motion. The presiding officer decides.
8. Close nominations: Purpose is to close nominations. It must be seconded, but cannot be discussed. A two-thirds vote is needed.

V. Unclassified Motions

A. Definition: Unclassified motions are those that are not classified above. These motions cannot be made if any other matter is pending.

B. Examples:

1. Take from the table: Brings up for consideration a previously tabled motion. It may be used after some other business has intervened but not later than the next meeting. A second is required; it is not debatable or amendable and needs a majority vote.
2. Reconsider: Must be made by a person who voted with the prevailing side of the motion. "I move to reconsider the motion that...." A second is required and a majority vote is needed. Generally, it is done later in the meeting after new facts have been presented but no later than the next regularly scheduled meeting.

Need more information? For sample charts that outline how to handle motions, see *Parliamentary Procedure Without Stress* by Roberta McDow or visit the parliamentarian association resources listed in Chapter 7.

METHODS OF VOTING

Voting is such a familiar experience at meetings that we usually accept its mechanics without questions, concentrating only on the issue the vote will decide. To protect our right to vote and to exercise it correctly, we also need to know something about the mechanics of voting.

Majority vote, two-thirds vote, and plurality vote are numerical descriptions of voting. Voice vote, rising vote, show of hands, ballot vote, machine vote, roll call, absentee vote, and general consent are all means of registering a vote. The phrase "two-thirds roll call vote" describes both the numerical requirement and the means.

Majority Vote. A majority is more than half. It could be further defined as "majority of the votes cast" or "majority of the membership."

Two-Thirds Vote. This vote requires that two-thirds of the votes cast are in favor of the motion. In general, a two-thirds vote is required to pass any measure that interferes with the rights of the members.

Plurality Vote. A plurality is the greatest number of votes for a candidate or a measure in a contest of three or more choices. It is possible, then, for a plurality to be less than a majority. If a majority vote is required, a plurality less than a majority cannot elect.

Voice Vote. This is the familiar aye and no vote.

Rising Vote. Members stand to register their vote in favor or opposition to the motion when asked. A rising vote can be demanded by a single member with a motion called Division of the Assembly.

Show of Hands. Voting by raising a hand is an alternative to the voice vote or the standing vote.

Ballot. The advantage of voting by ballot is that members enjoy the right of keeping their preferences secret. This is a time-consuming method of voting that is usually reserved for elections or some other important contest. The ballot can be any piece of paper on which the member writes his choice.

Machine Vote. This is a mechanical version of the ballot vote. It has the advantage of providing a fast and accurate means for counting the vote.

Roll Call. This method of voting records just how the members voted. It should not be used unless the members are representatives of other people who are entitled to know how their elected agents voted.

Absentee Vote. Normally this is a vote by mail. A similar provision is the vote by proxy where another member casts votes for the member. Neither of these is a practical option for in-school organizations.

General Consent. A great deal of time is saved in meetings by the use of general consent where the chair asks for corrections or objections to the issue being considered. By remaining silent, the members give their consent to the motion. General consent cannot be used to pass a main motion, elect officers, or decide other important issues. It is used when no opposition is apparent to a decision on a procedural matter. If someone objects, however, a vote must be taken by voice or other appropriate means.

STUDENT OFFICER ROLES IN PARLIAMENTARY PROCEDURE

1. Presiding officers: President and Vice-President
   - Call the meeting to order
   - Recognize members
   - Re-state questions
   - Announce results of voting
   - Decide on points of order
2. Secretary
   - Records facts, decisions
   - Puts items of business considered in writing
3. Treasurer
   - Reports on financial condition of the group
   - Advises on the amount of funds available for specific projects
4. Committee chairmen
   - Responsible to the group
   - Responsible for committee meetings
   - Responsible for committee reports
   - Responsible for tasks assigned by the group
5. Members
   - Are informed about the basic rules
   - Use the rules to the best advantage of the group
6. Parliamentarian
   - Helps the officers interpret the rules
   - Teaches rules to the group at the beginning of each year.

PARLIAMENTARY PROCEDURE GLOSSARY

Address the chair—to speak to the presiding officer.

Adjourn—to dismiss or end a meeting.

Agenda—a list of items to be done or dealt with at a meeting.

Amend—to change or modify a motion.

Ballot—to vote by casting a written ballot.

Chair—the presiding officer of the meeting.

Division of the house—a standing vote called for by a member.

Ex-officio—by virtue of office, as "The president is an ex-officio member of that committee."

House—the group, club or organization.

Lay question on the table—to put aside a motion for further consideration at another meeting.

Majority vote—the votes of more than half of the members present voting at the meeting (unless otherwise stated).

Meeting—a gathering of the organization's members.

Minutes—the record or report of work of each meeting kept by the secretary.

Make a motion—to propose a certain project be done by the organization. "I move that we...."

New business—business that has been brought up for the first time.

Nomination—suggesting the name of a person for an office to be used at a time of election. It is not a motion and requires no second.

Obtain the floor—to obtain the right to speak, with permission and recognition being given by the chairperson. No one may speak unless recognized by the chairperson.

Point of order—seeking to clarify or correct procedure or business.

Pro-tem—for the time being, as "He is secretary pro-tem, acting in place of the secretary who is absent."

The question or call for the question—the motion before the assembly. When members wish to close the discussion and put the matter to a vote they may "call the question."

Quorum—the number of members necessary to carry on the business. Refer to your organization's constitution for number for majority.

Refer to a committee—to put certain work in the hands of a small group of people who are better able to consider the matter than the whole organization. The committee must report its results at a later meeting.

PARLIAMENTARY PROCEDURE GLOSSARY

Second—an indication that at least a second person is in favor of discussing a motion. All motions must be "seconded."

Special committee—a committee appointed for some particular purpose.

Standing committee—a committee provided for in the constitution, usually appointed for one year.

Unfinished business—business that has been carried from a previous meeting.

Withdraw a motion—a motion permitting a previous motion to be withdrawn. It is not debatable and cannot be amended, but may be reconsidered.

ACTION PLANNING

Action planning combines commitment, collaboration, and ongoing efforts toward achieving the group's goals. Collaboration is a key element because people support what they help create and are more committed to ensuring the goals are achieved. The benefits of using an action plan (a work plan) to reach goals and solve problems include:

- It involves the people who make the change
- It invites people to invest interest, time, and responsibility in the outcome
- It keeps the input and atmosphere positive
- It dignifies people by accepting their input and assigns them responsibility for implementing the changes
- It continues the evaluation, revision, and change process
- It develops a starting point.

How does action planning work? The process is guided by a basic plan as outlined below:

MINI-ACTION PLAN

1. Problem. (Stated in terms of performance and behavior) "What does this problem do?"
2. Realistic idea. (What you want to see, stated in terms of performance) "Here's what we want to happen."
3. Obstacles. (Why isn't it already as you want it?) "What's getting in the way of..."
4. Resources. (People, money, time, knowledge to overcome obstacles) "Here's what'll help."
5. Intervention(s) or program plan selected. (What resources do you combine?) "Here are some ways to reach our goal."
6. Jobs. (Who does what and when?)
7. Next steps. (What happens now?) "Here's what I need to do."
8. And now. (What happened and what we need to do next) The group should have an action plan to address each important task or issue it is facing.

INTERACTION METHOD

The interaction method is designed to increase participation in meetings and to use available time effectively. This method encourages wider participation by the group and is particularly useful in smaller groups, such as committees. This style of meeting should be used when:

- You have a particular problem to solve and a formal meeting will not generate ideas
- You are looking for new or improved activities for your group
- Brainstorming is completed and you want to give in-depth attention to several ideas generated from brainstorming.

This method is guided by four main roles: facilitator, recorder, group members, and chairperson or president.

The facilitator. Keeps the group focused on the agenda, encouraging ideas from all members and chauffeuring the group toward its goals.

- Is a neutral servant of the group
- Does not evaluate or contribute ideas without permission by the group
- Focuses energy of the group on a common task
- Suggests alternative methods and procedures
- Protects individuals and their ideas from attack
- Encourages everyone to participate
- Helps the group find win–win solutions
- Coordinates pre- and post-meeting organization
- Makes a contract with the group. For example, "Hi, I'm Jane and I'm going to facilitate today's meeting. I will encourage your participation, keep you on track, keep you moving, and make suggestions about ways to attack a problem. I won't evaluate any idea or add my own. I'm just here to help you get through the agenda successfully. I need you to tell me when I'm not sticking to my contract. Are there any questions?"

Specific Techniques:

- Clearly define your role.
- Show the group an agenda and ask for revisions and additions.
- Get agreement on a common problem and process before beginning.
- Boomerang questions back to group members (e.g., "I don't know; what do you think?").
- Be positive—compliment the group.
- Accept corrections nondefensively.
- Don't talk too much.
- Support and keep the recorder in his or her role.
- Don't be afraid to make mistakes.
- Help educate the group.

The recorder. Keeps the record of all ideas (typically on butcher paper) and adds new suggestions as the meeting proceeds.

- Uses the words of the speaker. Does not edit or paraphrase.
- Records enough of the speaker's ideas so they can be understood later.
- Remains neutral like the facilitator and does not contribute his or her own ideas.
- Makes a contract with the group to perform the function to the best of his or her ability.
- Because the record of the meeting is within full view of the membership, it serves as a sort of group memory:
  - Helps the group focus on a task
  - Is an instant record of a meeting's content and process
  - Captures all ideas, freeing participants from taking notes
  - Depersonalizes ideas
  - Prevents repetition and wheel spinning
  - Encourages participation because it respects individuals' ideas
  - Enables group members to check to make sure their ideas are being recorded accurately
  - Increases group's sense of accomplishment
  - Makes it easy to catch up latecomers without interrupting the meeting
  - Makes accountability easier because decisions are written down in clear view of the group.

Specific Techniques:

- Listen for key words. Try to capture basic ideas, the essence. Use abbreviations.
- Accept corrections nondefensively.
- Print or write legibly and large enough so everyone can read.
- Write as quickly as possible.
- Don't be afraid to misspell.
- Use colored markers to highlight, divide ideas, underline.
- Use stars, arrows, numbers, dots, and so forth, to highlight ideas.
- Number and date all sheets.

Group members. Focus on the topic and actively participate and support others by staying open and positive. Group members have the following roles and responsibilities:

- To see that ideas are adequately recorded.
- To keep the facilitator and recorder neutral and out of the content discussion.
- To take responsibility for the success of the meeting.
- To use the same facilitative behaviors, tools, and techniques that the facilitator uses (protect people, encourage participation).
- To focus energy on the content of the problem.
- To respect and listen to other individuals. Protect others' points of view. Facilitate from your seat.

- To vary their seating pattern—avoid cliques.
- To let go of "idea ownership."
- To listen to all of what others say and to try to understand what they mean—ask questions.
- To try to keep an open mind.
- To paraphrase. Say what you like first!

Chairperson/president. Acts as part of the group, may express opinions, and can also make further assignments as discussion proceeds. The parliamentary restriction of neutrality is not expected when using the interaction method.

GROUP DISCUSSION

Group discussion is the pooling of the best information and the best thinking of the group in order to reach the best solution or to obtain the best information. To achieve these goals, participants must think straight, think for themselves, and be open-minded, considering all decisions tentative.

When preparing to discuss a problem, participants should organize their thoughts. To do that, they should:

- Be clear about the meanings of the terms of the topic under discussion.
- Analyze the problem. What is its extent, acuteness, effect? What are the causes? What are the goals? What tentative solutions are there? What are the advantages and disadvantages of these solutions? What suggestions are there for carrying out the proposed solution?

Group participants should also make three key resolutions:

1. To accept responsibility for doing their personal fair share
2. To prepare themselves so they can contribute effectively
3. To learn from each experience; to improve participation as the group progresses.

The participant must be conscious of the need for well-ordered group thinking and be able to discern the relationships among ideas. In addition, a good discussion participant is:

- Thoughtful, open-minded, and objective
- Forthright but tactful and temperate
- Sympathetically interested in the ideas of others
- Interested in promoting the common good
- An articulate speaker and active listener
- Curious
- Sincere
- Respectful of differences of opinion
- Able to identify and reduce points of actual disagreement to specific, clearly understood points
- Able to identify and remove points of misunderstanding that lie at the root of disagreements
- Able to promote agreement without compromising integrity.

Participants in group discussions should be courteous and respectful, speaking only when they have something relevant and useful to offer, not interrupting or monopolizing the discussion, being concise and specific.

GROUP DISCUSSION MODELS

Discussions can be formal and informal, structured and more free flowing. Two common types of discussions are roundtable discussions and panel discussions.

Roundtable Discussion. A roundtable discussion is a closed discussion with an informal organization. Members meet, with or without a chairman, and start talking. Their discussion may be structured, with an introduction and a conclusion, or it may be hit-or-miss.

Panel Discussion. A panel of participants is selected to carry on a discussion in front of and partially for the benefit of an audience. This usually is a relatively structured conversation guided by a designated facilitator, although it may be free-flowing as well. The audience may be allowed to ask questions or enter into the discussion while it is under way or after the panel has finished its own discussion.

HOW TO LEAD A DISCUSSION GROUP

Group discussion is a process focused on arriving at common understandings or a group decision. The method does not include argument or debate, but rather a group search for agreements or solutions. The final product is usually better than the best individual idea. The requirements of an effective group discussion are

- Quality leadership in guiding, inspiring, directing, and summarizing
- A group feeling of unity, common interest, friendliness, and willingness to share
- An open and accepting atmosphere
- A group working together toward common goals ... and sharing as they grow.

PREPARING FOR THE DISCUSSION GROUP

Understand the topic. Decide what areas should be considered and what should be left out. Plan an outline that covers the topics you want to discuss. Develop quality questions to guide the discussion.

- Arrive at the meeting room well ahead of the group. Arrange the chairs in a circle or such that every person will feel part of the discussion. Check lighting and ventilation.
- Welcome people as they arrive.

STARTING THE DISCUSSION

- Start on time.
- Announce the length of the session and briefly indicate how the time will be used. Do not wait for stragglers.
- Emphasize that this is a group in which everyone takes part, every view is expressed, and every opinion is respected. Each contribution is valuable. We learn together.
- See that every member knows every other member. At first meetings, it is good to have each person introduce him or herself. Learn the names of each person as soon as possible.
- Choose a recorder to keep notes of what is said, learned, and shared. Butcher paper on the wall with marking pens can provide a public memory of the discussion.

DURING THE DISCUSSION

Avoid the temptation to be the teacher or the expert. Ask questions, but draw answers out of the participants. Encourage others to express their opinions instead of expressing your own. Never say, "At my school, we ..." Be impartial—try to keep anyone from monopolizing or dominating (including yourself) and try to avoid showing disapproval of an idea. Encourage the expression of all ideas. Remain a member of the group, not the center but a facilitator, a chauffeur. Encourage members to talk with one another, not always to you.

Occasionally summarize what has been said. Be careful to invite the group's agreement on the summary, then redirect the group to the next topic of the discussion with a question. Don't rush the process. Clarify obscure contributions by tactfully asking for a restatement or restating the comment yourself and asking if your interpretation is accurate. Do I hear you say...?"

Encourage general participation by using such questions as, "How do the rest of you feel about this?" "Are there any other reactions to this idea?" "Does everyone feel that way?" If people begin to argue, thank them for their views and suggest tactfully that perhaps others would like to talk on this point. You may have to be firm and even interrupt the argument. Know that egos and emotions will surface.

Support anyone who seems to be embarrassed because their contribution meets with disapproval. Use a tactful comment such as "I can understand that point of view." It is important to look at every opinion. Encourage quiet people to enter the discussion by looking at them when you throw out a question to the group, inviting their reactions to someone else's comment. Avoid asking for facts or information they may not have because this may deter them from participating further.

Don't allow the discussion to meander. Move the group forward with a quick summary and transition question to a new topic. When people seem to be on a tangent, give them a little time, then ask the participants if they feel they're still "on the subject." Or, restate the question to get everyone focused and back on track.

Listen carefully to each contribution, absorbing the person's meaning, not just listening to the words. Some of the best questions you'll ask will come from careful listening and probing to get details or specific information. If conflicts occur, suggest that the conflict of ideas is desirable in good discussions but conflict of personalities is not. Guide people to consider the idea, not the person who contributed it.

Finish on time. Summarize what has been said as simply as possible and ask for the group's agreement on your summary. Give the group a feeling of accomplishment by suggesting that although there wasn't time for in-depth discussion or that no final answers were developed, the discussion yielded a quality exchange of ideas.

FOLLOW UP

During discussions you might notice that some people seem frustrated about their inability to find solutions to specific problems. Ask these people to share their problems with a member of the steering committee or offer to share them yourself.

Be aware of the tone of your group. If for some reason the group does not seem to gel, bring it up with other discussion leaders. Maybe a reshuffling of groupings is in order.

ALTERNATIVE MEETING STYLES

Maybe these types of meetings aren't what your group needs to address its issues. In that case, might opt for a form of interactional discussion. Interactional discussion is characterized by direct, easy interchange. Members speak up without waiting for formal recognition by the group leader, yet are aware of the other members and respectful of their contributions. Informational conferences, symposiums, buzz groups, cooperative investigation, house rules, lecture-presentation, open forums, and new technologies are forms of interactional discussion.

INFORMATIONAL CONFERENCE

An informational conference is a scheduled meeting at which all participants share their personal knowledge or experience to make the work of the group and its individual members more efficient. The goal of the informational conference is to produce information, not to isolate, examine, or solve a problem.

SYMPOSIUM

Several people, often experts in some aspect of the subject under consideration, are invited to make short speeches. When everyone has spoken, participants may ask questions or make statements about what another person said. The audience may be invited to join in.

BUZZ GROUP

After a general presentation or discussion or even prior to a program, the large group is divided into groups of six or eight persons. Each of these buzz groups is asked to consider a specific question related to the overall discussion. The small groups may be answering the same question, or each may examine a different question. Each group selects a leader and/or recorder. The time allowed for the discussion questions in the buzz group should be as short as possible to create a sense of urgency and importance. At the end of the allotted period, the leader of each buzz group presents the group's report to the whole assembly.

Every individual takes an active role in deliberation, even though contributions are filtered through the reporter. This process usually results in a noticeable increase in member interaction during and after the buzz session because every member feels as though he or she contributed to the discussion. The success of this method depends on the quality of questions assigned to each small group.

Buzz groups offer several advantages:

- Provide leadership opportunities to many students at once
- Offer early leadership experience over a small, manageable group
- Secure broad participation
- Stress responsibility
- Prevent same few students from hogging discussion in the large group
- Give the quiet, shy, isolated student a chance to contribute in a small group setting
- Provide movement and variety (large group to small group to large group)
- Give students the opportunity to speak in small groups and in large groups
- Stimulate discussion.

COOPERATIVE INVESTIGATION

Cooperative investigations are more formal than buzz sessions, and their purpose is more focused. They are designed for situations in which group members have limited if any information about the topic. There are usually eight steps to this "do it yourself" exercise.

1. The group meets in advance to elect a leader and to divide the topic into a number of subtopics. Members are assigned subtopics to investigate.
2. The leader calls one or more advance meetings to review assignments and assess progress.
3. At the beginning of the discussion meeting, the leader analyzes and defines the problem.
4. Each member presents his or her information in a brief report. The report contains only information, no argument.
5. When the reports are finished, the leader calls for any additional information.
6. The leader concludes the first portion of the meeting by summarizing the fresh pool of information and then opens the second half by inviting discussion in light of the facts presented.
7. If the nature of the problem permits, ways and means for putting an agreed-upon solution into operation are discussed.
8. At the conclusion of the discussion, the leader summarizes the points of agreement, identifies any problems that still need attention, and evaluates the process.

HOUSE RULES

Using house rules is an informal way to structure a meeting. House rules are usually 5 to 20 rules of courtesy and procedure that the group identifies for its own use. This method provides a simple, flexible framework for groups whose members want an alternative to strict parliamentary procedure.

House rules usually address the following areas:

- How will decisions be reached? Who makes them?
- How will ideas be presented? When? How many?
- How will ideas be changed?
- How will information be obtained?

LECTURE-PRESENTATION

The main purpose of a lecture-presentation is information sharing. Information is provided by qualified speakers well versed in the lecture topic. The speakers give their prepared remarks to the audience with little interaction from the rest of the group. An open forum on the topic follows the lecture.

OPEN FORUM

An open forum provides the opportunity for each group member to express an opinion about a topic. Each member has a right to speak; prepared or impromptu comments may be expressed freely. This information-sharing method lends itself to discussion of material from a movie, speech, or presentation. Order must be maintained and members are recognized by the leader in order to ensure that the forum process remains intact.

THREE GROUPING

Grouping students in threes provides a friendly orientation or welcome and enables students to get to know one another better. It is a way of breaking the ice and creating an informal environment to loosen people up. It is appropriate as a way to loosen people up or as a mixer technique. This configuration might be used for leadership classes; the first day of a class; camp sessions, church groups, or club meetings; homeroom, students council, or all-school meetings; or mixers or league meetings.

PRO-CON DISCUSSIONS

Using two or more presenters, present both sides and any alternative you can think of. Carefully define the issue and use a moderator to control the discussion. An additional person may be included to present alternatives or inject new points for consideration. Topics will be generated by the hot topics of the school or community but may include such questions as: Should we give school letters for academics and service? Is there a generation gap? Should students have curfews?

The controversial nature of some topics means that the moderator must establish ground rules and enforce them, chaperones should be on hand to ensure a well-mannered discussion, and presenters should stick to the facts.

NEW TECHNOLOGIES

Conference calls, chat rooms, communities of practice, blogs, and message boards are all forms of meetings. While not preferred by many who value face-to-face interaction, these meetings allow you to do business .

Meetings That Make Sense

By Michael Poll

Meetings—you love them, you hate them! On the one hand, they help us focus and motivate us to work on our plans. On the other hand, sometimes they seem boring and waste our time. We know what we want to accomplish but often lack the ability to be productive in spite of the meeting.

Often the problem is not the people attending the meeting or the lack of ideas and initiative; rather, it's the structure of the meeting itself. In organizations, meetings are held for various reasons. Those reasons should determine the type of meeting you host. In other words, the problem may be the way the meeting is being coordinated and facilitated.

Depending on the group and purpose of the meeting, it is important to realize what type of meeting is best. Not paying attention to this would be like trying to play baseball on a football field. The players are ready and the team is motivated to play as winners but the field doesn't have a home plate or a pitcher's mound! The same goes for your meetings: There is a time for informational meetings (where a facilitation style such as parliamentary procedure makes sense) and a time for idea generation meetings (where parliamentary procedure could stifle creativity)!

ALL MEETINGS ARE NOT CREATED EQUAL

Different types of meetings are designed to meet your specific needs. Following are meeting types most common to student leaders.

Brainstorming/Idea Generation Meetings

A brainstorming or idea generation meeting helps members develop new ideas for a specific purpose. This might be to develop a school dance theme, create new ways to help students interact more positively outside of class, or generate thoughts about how to help people cope with a tragedy that recently hit your community.

Generally, this type of meeting works best when everyone understands the basic ground rules of a brainstorming session. There are lots of resources on this, but basically, everyone is invited to contribute, all responses are considered, responses are not discussed or put down, and people are invited to generate and share crazy thoughts as a way of helping others spark their own ideas.

Brainstorming meetings are best used at the beginning of a group's desire to develop something or when a group is feeling that it is time to try something new. This type of meeting works because members know that their opinions will be considered and valued. People contribute and feel important when brainstorming is used correctly.

Team-Building Meetings

"We are already a team, why do we need a team-building meeting?" Well, is your group in conflict? Do members struggle with decision making issues? Are they prepared to work when it's time to roll up their sleeves and dive in? All groups go through cycles where they no longer function as the solid team they once were. As the school year begins, students sometimes feel alienated and consider leaving the group. When this occurs, often a team-building meeting is the cure.

A team building meeting helps members become connected to the group, whether or not the members or the team is new. You can take several approaches to team-building meetings. You basically want to arrange opportunities for group members to get acquainted or reacquainted with each other. There are many "icebreaker" and problem solving activities that you are likely aware of and there are many resources available. During one of your meetings, instead of carrying on with the usual work at hand, take time to break the cycle and hold a team building meeting. Other options would be to do this during a weekend or hold an extended afternoon meeting.

Don't be surprised if everyone is not totally enthusiastic about doing it—often this suggests there really is a problem and you are on the right track. The key is to implement activities that meet the group where they are. In other words, if your group is struggling with understanding its purpose, a team building activity to help members learn each other's names isn't what you need. Be sure to consult with leadership resources available. Team building meetings are effective because they help members learn about each other as people, rather than just focusing full force on the group goals. By doing so, when it comes time to discuss group issues, the team is ready to communicate.

Weekly Focused Agenda Meetings

Most of us are familiar with focused agenda meetings. These are the meetings we attend on a regular basis. We discuss activities, learn about upcoming issues, and provide updated reports. These meetings typically follow parliamentary procedure: group members follow a set of standards that allow the facilitator (often the president or chairperson) to lead the group in discussion.

Parliamentary procedure works well, but there are two issues to consider. First, it is easy to get caught up in the details of using the procedures correctly. Do not allow that to happen. After all, you are not running the U.S. Senate. Use the procedures as a basic template to run your meeting. Help others learn good citizenship by following the procedures and observing various organizational meeting traditions. Second, parliamentary procedure is often overused when a different meeting leadership style (such as the examples in this article) is more appropriate. Parliamentary procedure is effective because the set procedures consist of a template that everyone can follow easily. It's not brain surgery once you understand the basics. These procedures help keep everyone on track and the meeting running smoothly.

Informational Meetings

Informational meetings offer an opportunity for people to share information, opinions, or data pertinent to the topic at hand. Suppose you ask committees to work and present information to the full group by a certain date, or give candidates running for office an opportunity to share their viewpoints with other students. These are examples of informational meetings.

Informational meetings follow a basic format of introducing the person(s) who will speak as well as the topic. Be sure to remind the presenter(s) of the amount of time allocated to them. This is perhaps the most significant problem with informational meetings: People talk too much!

Informational meetings are effective because people come to the meeting prepared to listen and learn about an issue. People know they will likely not be called on to make a decision right away unless this is determined in advance. Those sharing the information will be delighted because others will listen and possibly ask some clarifying questions. Having people listen to you in this manner creates positive energy and helps those sharing information feel appreciated.

Action/Decision Making Meetings

Everyone wants to take action and "make it happen" but some meetings seem to drain us of our energy and enthusiasm. Action or decision making meetings are designed to help us make decisions and provide a plan for us to go for it. They let people know that a decision has been made and that group members are empowered to do the work to make team goals come true—even if that means making posters and banners to promote your event! Action meetings may be facilitated in a semi-formal parliamentary format. The key is not to become so stifled, allowing little discussion, creativity, or decision making flexibility.

Create an agenda that lets the team know you will be discussing a topic and that a decision on their part is expected. On that agenda, write down the topic, who is presenting it, and the purpose. The purpose lets members know that a decision is required (DR) or a decision is preferred (DP). This communicates to the group that they should pay attention.

Next, place a time limit for the agenda item. This ensures that the person presenting the information has a set limit in which to do so and the possible question and answer period will not drag on. Finally, leave space on the agenda so members can write down the action steps that they and others are responsible for. This almost always ensures a high level of commitment!

Action/decision making meetings are effective because people come to them with the understanding that something, whether they agree with a decision or not, is going to happen. Also, students know they have an impact on that decision. If facilitated properly, people know the meeting will be a good use of their time and realize that they take part in implementing the actions that follow the meeting.

Problem Solving Meetings

Let's face it, from time to time your group will face problems. They may involve the group itself (low attendance, lack of motivation) or issues related to your group fulfilling its goals (lack of funds, change of school district policy). Problem solving meetings focus your attention directly on the issue. It is easy to pretend a problem doesn't exist or to ignore issues that only affect the group occasionally. Challenge those problems with a problem solving meeting.

The goal here is to collect information, make suggestions to work through the problem, and take necessary action. The meeting should enable students to share information in a productive, nonthreatening manner. Be sure that everyone understands the problem and writes it down. Develop suggestions or strategies for resolution. Depending on the issue and the level of comfort, trust, and knowledge within your group, you can do this in several ways. Some suggestions include brainstorming, involving everyone in open group discussions, bringing a subject matter expert to your meeting to discuss the issues regarding a specific problem, or having students individually reflect on the topic and submit written suggestions. Group members need to be supportive of each other; be sure to establish and reinforce meeting ground rules in the beginning.

The key advantage of this type of meeting is that students will focus on a particular issue. They should understand that they have the responsibility of solving this problem by doing their homework, creating a shared understanding of the issue, and developing solutions. Arguing and complaining won't help solve anything. Setting ground rules in the beginning helps group members let their guard down and encourages honesty and creativity.

MAKING MEETINGS WORK

When I present a popular program to students called Making Meetings Work for Student Leaders, I am often asked, "How do I know what kind of meeting I should be holding?" Truthfully, it's not always easy. Sometimes, especially in the beginning of the year, you know the group will need more brainstorming or idea generation meetings, but when the year gets busy you may need to focus and that calls for an action/decision making meeting. You will always have the need for weekly focused agenda meetings. When a topic comes up that may require a different type of meeting in order to successfully accomplish the task or deal with a specific need, suggest a meeting type that makes sense to address the issue. You may hold it during your next planned weekly meeting, arrange for an additional meeting, or, discuss the issue right then by establishing a time limit and ground rules for the type of meeting necessary.

Knowing what type of meeting will best suit your needs is key to meeting success. All of the idea generation, strategy development, creative brainstorming, conflict resolution, and group team building will come as a result of choosing and implementing the correct meeting type.

Michael Poll is a national speaker and trainer. Reprinted from *Leadership for Student Activities*.

Parliamentary Procedure: An Essential Skill

By M. Eugene Bierbaum

Most of my years in public education included the teaching of parliamentary procedure, and I am constantly confounded by the resistance to including this academic subject as a core requirement in the public schools. The resistance I have encountered may be the result of several misconceptions regarding the nature of parliamentary procedure.

Parliamentary procedure is none of the following:

A form of protocol. Although parliamentary procedure does involve some protocol (such as how members address the chair), that is not its primary purpose. Protocol is only "window dressing"; parliamentary procedure addresses the substance of meeting procedures.

A collection of rules. Parliamentary procedure is often regarded as a mere collection of rules. It is not. It teaches basic principles of group decision making, and those who understand the principles are able to apply the rules intelligently. All rules have some exceptions, and there are situations in which accepted rules do not apply.

An impediment to progress. Some people believe that progress could be made more quickly in meetings by dispensing with parliamentary procedure. The reverse is true. Failure to follow parliamentary procedure often impedes and obstructs the decision making progress.

A "bag of tricks." Parliamentary procedure is sometimes thought to consist of tricks that enable knowledgeable individuals to take advantage of their fellow members. On the contrary, it protects the rights of all members. Parliamentary procedure is the ultimate equalizer that treats all members exactly the same.

Why Teach Parliamentary Procedure?

If parliamentary procedure is none of the above, what is it and why should it be taught?

Parliamentary procedure teaches respect for the democratic decision-making process. Groups too often wait until a crisis arises to address the problems inherent in their decision making. The appropriate time to teach parliamentary procedure is before a crisis occurs. Parliamentary procedure provides a sound basis for democratic decision making that avoids floundering from one crisis to the next.

Parliamentary procedure expedites business. Meetings conducted according to parliamentary procedure move more quickly and get the required business done in less time. Because of this, many businesses (where "time is money") have begun to use the principles of parliamentary procedure in their meetings.

Meetings that follow parliamentary procedure are more focused and orderly. Parliamentary procedure allows only one item of business to be considered at any given time. All lines of communication are directed to and from the chair. There is less confusion and a much greater sense of order and accomplishment because members are able to follow the progress of the meeting.

Parliamentary procedure protects the rights of both the majority and the minority. The majority has the right to prevail on any given issue and the right to reasonable expediency in arriving at a decision. The minority has the right to be heard and the right to attempt to persuade others to accept its viewpoint (thus converting a temporary minority into a majority). Parliamentary procedure provides the tools for protecting both majority and minority rights so that no faction is allowed to arbitrarily impose its will on any other group.

Parliamentary procedure provides a common language for democratic decision making. To be effective in meetings, members must learn to speak the language of parliamentary procedure. Like any other language, this requires constant practice. Once mastered, the language of parliamentary procedure enables participants to meet on common ground and to deliberate in terms that are universally accepted as a basis for sound decision making.

The net result of using parliamentary procedure is a better informed citizenry capable of participating in the daily decision making that forms the basis of our democracy.

M. Eugene Bierbaum is professor emeritus of communication studies at the State University of New York.

Thirty-Minute Meetings That Work

By Mary Dee Schmidt

How many times have you sat through a seemingly endless meeting that ended with nothing being accomplished? In the busy lives of student leaders, finding time when everyone can meet is hard enough without wasting that time in ineffective meetings. When you do meet, it's important that the time you have be used to best advantage.

The American Youth Foundation developed a practical meeting plan for its Youth Leadership Compact Teams that calls for a 30-minute meeting once a week. The meetings are held in the same place, usually on the same day, and at the same time, so members can get in the routine of attending. The format for the meetings is the same each week. Before the meeting, the person who will facilitate meets with the adviser to set the agenda. During the meeting, a recorder uses the 30-minute meeting form to note what actually occurs. These forms are filed in a notebook for future reference. The recorder at one meeting becomes the facilitator for the next meeting. This way, the responsibility for facilitating meetings is shared among group members, and all gain experience as facilitators.

The meetings begin with 5 minutes of small talk. This provides time for everyone to gather, relax, and get their chit-chat out of the way so they can concentrate on the business at hand. After a call to order, 10 minutes is spent reporting on past actions. The group then turns to future actions and spends 10 minutes discussing what needs to be done and who needs to do it.

The 4 remaining minutes are spent reflecting on the process used. AYF calls this part "claiming," and it is an integral part of the learning experience. A "process observer" reports on how the group worked together. The process observer can be one of the group members or the adviser, and he or she concentrates on answering the question "how did we work as a team and individuals?" Teenagers don't often reflect on the big picture and look for patterns, so they keep repeating the same mistakes. Noting that certain people dominated the meeting, that suggestions were overlooked, or that some members opted not to participate in discussion can help the group become more aware of group process and function more effectively in the future.

However, this shouldn't be a time for criticism only. The process observer also reports on positive behaviors observed, such as the facilitator seeking opinions of those not volunteering them, keeping the group on task, etc. The process observer role is important as a learning tool for the group. It reminds members that it's not just the doing that is important; reflecting on how we do the work helps us learn lessons that can be applied in the future.

The basic tenet of AYF's Youth Leadership Compact program is that students can promote positive, tangible change in their schools through their training as peer leaders. The 30-minute meeting format provides a time-friendly tool for getting members in the habit of working in an organized fashion and keeps the team on track.

30-MINUTE MEETING FORMAT

I. Small Talk (5 minutes)

II. Call to Order (1 minute)

III. Past Actions/Tasks to be reported on (10 minutes)

What action?

What task?

A.

B.

C.

IV. Future Action/Tasks to be discussed (10 minutes)

What was discussed/decided?

Who's responsible?

Deadline

A.

B.

C.

V. Claiming (4 minutes)

Next meeting:

Location:

Recorder:

Date/Time:

Process observer:

Facilitator:

Mary Dee Schmidt is the director for youth leadership at Focus St. Louis (MO).

Parliamentary Rights: How Not To Get Pushed Around with Parliamentary Procedure

The Rank and File Member

The rank and file member usually does not learn parliamentary procedure. He or she leaves that to chairmen, to ambitious members who aspire to office, and to natural-born hecklers. One difficulty with this passive attitude is that sometimes the ordinary member gets pushed around. This may be due to dictatorial chairmen, an aggressive minority group, or to the victim's unfamiliarity with parliamentary usage. Here we review some of the ways in which members may protect their rights.

Rights That Should Not Be Protected

If the member wants to compel the group to listen all night to his or her views, read no further. This will not tell you how to guarantee that right. If you want to prevent the majority from carrying out their wishes, no matter how ill-advised, you will find no help in here either.

The Right to Appeal

If the chairman rules against you, and if you honestly think he or she was wrong, you have a right to appeal the decision of the chair. Better have the documentation to support your contention. This or some other authoritative manual will do if you know how to find the citation in a hurry. You may even interrupt someone else to make this appeal, though it is discourteous to do that if it can be avoided. But your appeal must have a seconder. If there is not even one other member who agrees with you, yours is a lost cause. You may not use an appeal as a substitute for reconsideration or as a wedge for reopening a discussion on the merits. You use it when you sincerely think the chair has made a parliamentary mistake.

The Right to an Explanation

If you think someone is pulling a fast one by double talk or jargon, you rise to a "point of information." You are entitled to an explanation of the meaning of a motion and you use the "point of information" to get it. Do not use a "point of information" as a platform for discussing the merits of a question. If you need explanation about a parliamentary or procedural point, you raise a "point of parliamentary inquiry."

Freedom from Insult

Unless you are the defendant in a formal disciplinary action, you are immune from charges of dishonesty, venal motives, stupidity, or disloyalty. If you are defamed, you may interrupt the speaker by rising to a "point of order."

Right To Have the Agenda Followed

A group may try to put something over by removing an item from its place on the agenda and voting on it at a time favorable to them. They cannot get away with this if a few other members are alert.

The way to enforce this right—or get a clear statement from two-thirds of the members that they don't want to enforce it—is by a call for "orders of the day." If they want to, two-thirds of the group can vote to suspend the rules and thus take something up out of order. And if two-thirds of the group doesn't agree with you, you don't have many rights left, anyway.

Preventing an Unrepresentative Majority from Binding the Organization

If you think that a meeting is highly unrepresentative, you may prevent irrevocable action. You do this by a motion to reconsider later. In some manuals this is called a "Motion To Reconsider and Enter on the Minutes." You need a second, and the delay is only until the next meeting. But you may believe that a more representative group will come to the next meeting.

Right to Talk

This is a qualified right. If two-thirds of those present want to stop debate they can do it by a motion to that effect. And when that is done, you have no right to talk. If you made the main motion in the first place, you do have an absolute right to speak to it, provided you ask for the floor as soon as it is seconded, and provided the motion is a debatable one. If someone who has already discussed a matter is again clamoring for the floor while you have not yet been recognized, you may rise to a point of order if the chair recognizes that person and ignores you. As a rule, a member is not permitted to talk a second time to a motion if a previously silent member is asking for the floor. If the chair refuses to recognize you, you may appeal. Once you have spoken, however, the chair is within its rights in refusing to let you talk again if some previously silent member wants the floor.

While talking, you may be interrupted by any member who raises a point of privilege or who wants to appeal a recently announced decision. If you are first speaker on the motion, you may be interrupted by an "objection to consideration." Otherwise, no one but the chairperson may interrupt you; and he/she may interrupt only if you are becoming tangential in topic, abusive in manner, or highly repetitive. If the chair insists that you have talked long enough, or says your discussion is out of order for any reason, you must either conform to the request or ask for an appeal.

Right to Stop Someone Else from Talking

If the speaker is really out of order, you may interrupt by a "point of order." Otherwise you have to wait until you can get a word in and then make a motion to stop debate, to lay on the table, to refer it to a committee, or to adjourn. Any of these motions, if seconded, would have to be disposed of before debate on the primary motion could continue.

Right to Reopen a Matter

A meeting cannot be compelled to act on the same subject time and time again just because a few members keep returning to it. However, most primary motions can be renewed if some other business has intervened; and any member who voted on the prevailing side may, under certain circumstances, move to reconsider action just taken.

The Right to Exclude Outsiders

Sometimes a member feels tongue-tied in the presence of strangers and wants to feel free to discuss a matter with only members in the room. This is done by moving to go into executive session.

The Right to Have Your Motion Seriously Considered

A member cannot resent his or her motion's being defeated; he or she recognizes that the majority has that right. But he or she resents a maneuver that keeps the group from clearly voting on his or her motion one way or the other. The devices to prevent your motion from reaching a clean decision are:

Objection to reconsideration
Laying on the table

Postponing indefinitely
Postponing to a definite time
Referring to a committee
To attach a stultifying amendment
To adjourn.

When Objection to Consideration Is Raised

This motion is not in order if debate has gotten beyond the first speaker. If the "objection" is then raised, and if the chairman entertains it, the maker rises to a point of order and suggests that the motion is out of order. If the motion is made in good time, there must be a vote on it. But it takes a two-thirds vote to kill the matter. If two-thirds of the voters want to take the matter off the agenda, there is nothing the maker of the motion can do about it at that time. After some other business has intervened, he or she may move to reconsider the vote which withdrew his or her subject from the floor. To make such a motion, he or she must have voted with the two-thirds majority in the first place.

When a Matter Is Laid on the Table

Someone hostile to your motion may move to lay it on the table. If seconded, the motion to lay on the table is immediately (without debate) voted on. If passed (and a majority vote is sufficient) the matter is put on the shelf. You may not move to reconsider a vote to lay on the table.

If Indefinite Postponement Is Moved

If this motion passes, your subject is practically dead; debate stops, and you cannot revive the matter at this meeting. You can

Debate it fully and perhaps convince the group to defeat the motion to postpone indefinitely.

Move to refer the matter to a committee. If it passes, then you have at least kept the matter alive and can appeal to the committee.

If this fails, your third device is to move to postpone to a definite time. If this passes, it ensures that the matter will come up again at the time specified. If that fails, the fourth possibility is to lay the whole matter on the table. Finally, if all this fails, your fifth and last recourse is to let the motion pass, voting for it yourself; and then, as soon as you get the floor thereafter, moving to reconsider.

If Motion Is Made to Postpone to a Definite Time

It is usually good tactics to let this motion take its course.

When Threatened with Adjournment

If the organization really wants to adjourn, you can't stop it.

The Right to a Secret Vote

If you represent a group of members, you have no right to a secret vote. However, at a general membership meeting, you have a right to keep your vote a secret on at least two occasions:

On Voting for Office or Voting on Disciplinary Matters

For these occasions, a secret ballot, i.e., a printed ballot that does not request the voter's name, can and should be used.

Right to Change Your Vote

Any member may change his or her unwritten vote up to the time the chair announces the results.

The Right to a Recess

You have a right to ask for, but not insist on, a recess.

How Not to Get Pushed Around

Listed here are the ways in which an unsophisticated member may be deprived of some parliamentary rights, and points up the methods for meeting this challenge. If the meeting is overwhelmingly determined to deprive the member of a right, they can do it by simply sustaining the chairperson. Usually, however, it is a matter of unfamiliarity with the procedure rather than deliberate malice. Hence a copy of *Parliamentary Procedure Without Stress* or some authoritative manual of procedure should be at hand.

By Earl Reum
Adapted from *Meetings That Matter* (1993).

Plan: Planning a Meeting

"The first consideration when planning a meeting is whether or not one is required."
—Marion E. Haynes, author, meetings expert

Although meetings take many forms and serve many purposes, each should be planned carefully to ensure the goals of the meeting are realized. When planning the meeting, keep these things in mind:

Purpose. Every meeting must have a purpose that is acceptable to its participants. If there is no real purpose, there shouldn't be a meeting! Sometimes the purpose is clearly stated; sometimes it's taken for granted. Do you want people to experience something? Learn something? Make decisions? Plan something? Structure your meeting to accomplish its purpose.

People. Consider who will be present at the meeting. Are they familiar with the business at hand? How motivated will they be to participate? Answering these questions will help determine the format and the agenda of the meeting.

Setting. The meeting location should promote participation and productivity. Choose your meeting location based on the following seven Ss of site selection:

1. Size—How many can be seated? Will the area accommodate every person expected to attend the meeting?
2. Sound—Can everyone hear easily? Is a PA system needed?
3. Sight—Can everyone see the speakers and facilitators? When materials are displayed for view, can everyone see them?
4. Supplies—butcher paper, markers, notepads?
5. Schedules—Will the school require schedule modifications to accommodate student movement to and from the event if you're holding the event on campus during the school day?
6. Safety—Is the meeting site physically safe? Must you address any security matters, particularly for after-school or evening meetings?
7. Supervision—Who is ultimately responsible for supervising the group? Is additional building supervision necessary? To whom does the meeting supervisor need to report?

Time. The meeting length depends on the purpose, agenda, and time available. Plan your agenda so that everything that needs to be accomplished can be accomplished within the time allowed.

Agenda. One of the most important elements of a successful meeting is a well-planned agenda. An agenda is a written outline of plans for the meeting, developed with officers and members, that lists the order in which items are addressed during the meeting. The agenda should be flexible so if necessary, members can agree to modify the order of business or the items discussed. The typical meeting agenda includes the following in order:

- Call to order
- Roll call
- Reading and approving minutes from the last meeting
- Reports of officers, starting with the treasurer
- Reports of committees: standing and special
- Unfinished business
- New business
- Announcements and reminders
- Program, feature presentation, speaker
- Adjournment.

The agenda should focus on the needs of students and outline student leaders' responsibilities for managing the meeting. (See sample agenda and planning exercise in Chapter 7)

Evaluation. After the meeting, take time to evaluate its success. What constitutes success for your meeting? Did the meeting support your group goals? Did the participants, location, or time influence its success or lack of success? What might have made the meeting more successful?

TIPS FOR REGULAR MEETINGS

Many groups meet once a week. These quick tips can help ensure that these regular meetings are productive.

1. Establish a regular, consistent meeting location. Find the best room possible for your meetings. A quiet, well-ventilated room with good lighting in a central location is ideal.
2. Stock the room with appropriate materials such as office supplies, butcher paper, pencils, staplers, a calendar, computer, telephone, tape, and markers. Restock as necessary so you aren't left without necessary materials for any meeting.
3. Know how to set up a microphone if you are planning to use one.
4. Appoint someone to be responsible for the room and its equipment.
5. Keep a resource folder that includes faculty names, home phone numbers of group members, speakers, suppliers, school business partners, and more.

MEETING PLANNING CHECKLIST

In the early stages of planning the meeting, take the following items into consideration to ensure a productive session. List the tasks (revised the suggested tasks listed below to suit your needs) and include space for the meeting coordinators to assign tasks to the individuals who are helping with meeting preparation.

- ❑ Members are notified well in advance the time, date, and location of the meeting.
- ❑ Letters of invitation are sent to guest speakers or other non-members who are to attend the meeting. Include directions to the meeting location.
- ❑ An agenda is planned and copies are prepared for attendees.
- ❑ People who will be leading activities or presenting information during the meeting are notified and understand what is expected of them.
- ❑ Committee reports or other handouts are ready and copied for participants
- ❑ The room is reserved.
- ❑ Necessary equipment (microphone, computer, video player, etc.) is hooked up and tested to make sure it works.
- ❑ Layout of the room is checked to make sure it is conducive to the planned activities.
- ❑ Room set-up arrangements are made and the appropriate number of chairs and tables are determined.
- ❑ Custodial requests are made.
- ❑ Name tags are purchased.
- ❑ Copies of previous minutes are prepared.
- ❑ Visual aids are prepared.
- ❑ Refreshments are ordered.
- ❑ Meeting evaluation form is prepared.
- ❑ Students are asked to serve as greeters to welcome attendees to the meeting.
- ❑ Other:

WHO DOES WHAT? PARTICIPANTS' RESPONSIBILITIES

When planning a meeting, be sure each participant understands his or her responsibilities. With everyone working together, the meeting will be more productive. Go over these responsibilities with the key students:

OFFICERS

- Know group goals
- Serve those they represent
- Work constantly
- Provide leadership
- Plan the meeting
- Share!

Before the Meeting:

- Choose meeting goals
- Determine the kind of meeting to hold
- Plan the agenda and distribute copies
- Check the meeting place for chairs and working equipment
- Arrive on time
- Be ready to help.

During the Meeting:

- Help to get started on time
- Follow the agenda
- Help with the discussion
- Know the proper procedure to get things done
- Encourage members, giving each a chance to participate
- Make positive suggestions
- Listen to each person
- Help summarize progress and keep the meeting on track
- Use the last few minutes to summarize and highlight important decisions.

After the Meeting:

- Put the room back in order
- Evaluate the meeting
- List accomplishments
- Take on jobs to do
- Check the minutes and reports

- Send the minutes out
- List items to do
- Check committee work and reports
- Follow up on recommendations and action
- Prepare the next agenda
- Do the work
- Investigate and report on items of interest.

MEMBERS

- Know group goals and choose them
- Serve those they represent
- Work constantly
- Give reports
- Collect and bring ideas to meetings.

Before the Meeting:

- Review the agenda
- Be sure all needed materials are ready
- Arrive on time.

During the Meeting:

- Help the group set the order of events
- Listen attentively, respectfully, and participate
- Help keep the group on the subject
- Take notes to help recall information later
- Help keep the group to its time limits for each item
- Use written motions so everyone may have a copy
- Be sure everyone has a chance to talk
- Keep asking: Did we reach our goals for the meeting? Did we use our people and materials well? Did we waste time "trying to solve the impossible"?

After the Meeting:

- Read the distributed copies of the minutes
- Make a report to those you represent as soon as possible
- Write down important ideas and reactions to bring to the next meeting.

The plans are all laid out. The group members have arrived. What skills do you need to conduct your meeting with style and effectiveness?

Nametags: More Than Identification

By Mike Smith

Nametags are a familiar item that many people think of for situations in which participants don't know each other's names. But a simple nametag can serve many other useful purposes and can help solve some common meeting problems.

Situation 1: Not Everyone Participates.

In any crowd of more than 10 people, usually at least 7 are not good at remembering names. Set those people in a meeting of people who are good at remembering names and they feel uncomfortable and are therefore unlikely to participate. Many good ideas are lost for lack of expression. How can we create a comfortable situation for everyone and begin to capitalize on those usually unspoken good ideas?

Tip: Require nametags. Sales people are taught that the single most important sound to any human being is the sound of his or her own name. Don't assume that members know each other. Within a class they might, but do the seniors know the freshmen? Helping your membership remember each other's names and use them will improve your internal communication.

By creating attractive nametags and requiring their use, your members need not suffer from the discomfort of not knowing names. Permanent, creative nametags for regular members and "guest tags" for visitors set a positive tone in your meeting. The most important nametag design feature is a very large first name or in computer language, name-to-use, the name the wearer wants to be called. (Robert might go by Bob. Use Bob.) Group participation will increase because your members and guests will not feel intimidated by poor memory. You will be surprised at the new atmosphere in your meeting and the increase in productivity.

Situation 2: Roll Taking Creates Hard Feelings.

Have you been in meetings in which the person taking roll mispronounced several members' names? Didn't that create an uncomfortable atmosphere and set a negative tone for the meeting?

Tip: Put the nametags on the seats before the meeting. Those people whose tags are still on the seats when the meeting begins are absent. No more mispronouncing last names at the start of a meeting.

Situation 3: Our Members Gather into Cliques and Factionalize.

Cliques are a part of life, formed and reinforced by proximity. That is to say, where we sit at the first meeting of any group often determines the cliques we join. If left to make the decision ourselves we are bound by some "code" to sit next to someone we already know. Constantly sitting together solidifies those relationships and creates cliques. We then tend to feel the need to protect our fellow cliquers from the "others." We grow to defend "our" ideas and to close our minds to the ideas of others. That is factionalism.

Cliques themselves are not bad, but the factionalism they can generate can be counterproductive. Arguments in meetings are often disagreements between factions rather than disagreements about issues. How can we avoid this factionalism and strengthen the team feeling for the entire group?

Tip: Use your nametags to move all members every meeting. Meetings are improved and team building is enhanced when you take the time to control where your members sit at each meeting. Simply keep a seating chart. Place the nametags on the seats and have the members sit where their tags are. Please explain the reason for the moves and ensure you use the chart for every meeting. The object is to have every member sit with every other member several times in the course of the year. Using the nametag and other ice breaking skills will strengthen your efforts at team building.

Nametags can help you build your team and can help you improve the performance of your group. When planning your next meeting, don't forget the nametags!

How Meetings Can Get More Out of You

By Earl Reum

- Don't just drop ideas—do something with each suggestion as it arrives.
- Don't get involved in "sidepocket" conversations or clique critiques.
- Be your own tough parliamentarian. Expect it of others, too.
- Stick to the agenda—try to get everything accomplished in order as the agenda indicates.
- Respect each other person—even if he or she disagrees with what you just said.
- Listen to the speaker—concentrate and try to understand what he or she is saying.
- Take notes at every meeting. Organize them for rapid reference. Read them regularly.
- Take a stand on issues—prove to yourself you have the guts to do it.
- Give less experienced members a chance to speak.
- Don't be a jellyfish and let the loudmouths make the decisions.
- Assertive or aggressive behavior may be a necessary procedure.
- Be friendly, actively participate. People respond to honest warmth.
- Give different opinions a chance to be heard. Seek honesty—not just "my way."
- Keep meetings orderly—one thing at a time, in logical order, with majority rule deciding and with the understanding of every person.
- Don't just hear what you think you hear—check it out.
- If you're not sure what someone meant by his or her last remark, ask.
- Don't be afraid to admit you're wrong.
- Don't take anyone for granted—including yourself.
- Be actively interested in what's going on—or perhaps what should.
- Sleep at home—not during meetings! Be interested—get excited.
- Assume that other people are actively involved in getting things done—and join them.

By Earl Reum
Adapted from *Meetings That Matter* (1993).

Do: Conducting a Meeting

"People say, 'So many meetings, no results,' but no, that's not the point. Having so many meetings gives you comfort with each other and you are able to exchange views frankly, you are able to know each other better."

—Sellapan Ramanathan, president of Singapore

Good planning is essential for an effective meeting, but it's only the first step. What happens during the actual meeting is just as important. Here are some characteristics of a good meeting in process:

- The purpose of the meeting is clearly communicated.
- Only items that can be handled in the time allowed for the meeting are on the agenda.
- Someone is recording the ideas presented and decisions made and will get copies of those notes to everyone after the meeting.
- No single person dominates the meeting; everyone is encouraged to participate.
- Real issues are presented and are handled honestly. If people believe there are hidden agendas, they are encouraged to bring comments into the open.
- Only one issue or subject is handled at a time.
- A solution is not reached until the problem has been adequately discussed and analyzed. Premature motions divide the group and create artificial disagreements.
- Decision making procedures are clear ahead of time. (Will we take a majority vote? Will we reach consensus?)
- The meeting leader shows no bias and encourages everyone to participate.
- All agreements made during the meeting are recapped at the end of the meeting.

Keys for Successful Meetings: Experienced advisers who have worked with secondary level students will quickly tell you that there are three key elements to making your meeting a success with young people: both genders are present, food is available, and music is included somewhere in the meeting. Consider including these elements in some appropriate fashion at your next meeting.

GETTING YOUR MEETING STARTED

1. Arrange chairs to serve the goals of the meeting. Use a circle, semicircle, or square arrangement so members can see each other. Try to keep away from windows and doors to avoid distractions.
2. Have paper, pencils, agendas, handouts, and a large calendar ready. Print the goals for the meeting on the agenda. Create and laminate a poster that states the group's basic goals and post it at every meeting.
3. Start on time. End on time. Announce your policy at the first meeting, and then keep to it.
4. Agree on the ground rules. Is the group so large that members should rise when speaking? Can members speak without raising their hands? Do facilitators present their verbal contracts at the beginning of each meeting? What processes can we use during what parts of meetings? Does everyone understand and agree to such procedures?
5. Follow the agenda, agreeing that changes may be made with the group's consent during the course of the meeting.

MANAGEMENT STRATEGIES FOR MEETING LEADERS

1. Place yourself where everyone can see you.
2. Be aware of how you present yourself. Your voice and posture indicate your confidence. People respond to these things.
3. Stay neutral. Do not allow put downs or asides among members. Be sure that all comments are relevant to the topic.
4. Do not let meetings drag. Stick to the agenda. Move business along when discussion gets repetitious.
5. Listen to what is being said. If you perceive strong currents of disagreement or indecision, suggest compromises or appoint committees to report back with a plan.
6. Above all, be well-informed about every topic on the agenda so you can ask questions and draw out information the group needs to make intelligent decisions.

The meeting leader:

- Knows all members by name, using place cards or name tags to help remember
- Is at ease and comfortable in the position of leadership
- Is not too aggressive

- Is a good communicator, speaking properly and effectively
- Uses proper meeting procedures
- Delegates to members special jobs
- Ask members for opinions and ideas
- Encourages discussion
- Summarizes the discussion when necessary
- Gives directions but does not dictate
- Is not afraid to say, "I don't know, but we'll find out."
- Uses guides provided by the adviser.

FACILITATING A MEETING

Much of the success of an effective meeting can be attributed to a leader who has mastered skills of presiding. Keep these points in mind when presiding over a meeting:

1. Present the discussion as a quest rather than a debate. Everyone, including the leader, should expect to come away from the meeting with more information than he or she brought.
2. Avoid arguments over technicalities. Do not permit members to profess a particular point of view just for the sake of argument. If the matter is worth discussing to begin with, that means there are already differences of opinion.
3. At the beginning of the discussion, share with the group members a rough outline of the process so they will feel that they know where they are going in terms of process rather than outcome. Present questions that may be explored rather than answers that must be attained.
4. Realize that the responsibility to initiate discussion lies with the facilitator.
5. Keep your eyes open to nonverbal cues.
6. Avoid tangles over words and definitions. Focus on overall messages rather than the individual terms used to express it.
7. Draw out shy people with friendly encouragement.
8. Give brief statements, not speeches. You want to stimulate a rapid give-and-take of information so everyone has an opportunity to contribute. You don't need to comment on every statement made by group members.
9. Summarize often to keep members focused on the topic. You role is to orient and guide. When the group comes to a decision about an issue, make it clear that no more discussion is needed on that point.
10. Recognize that being a leader does not make you a "gifted" individual who knows all the answers. Your leadership is a service to the group—but the emphasis is on the group. Handle business by general consent.
11. Work for consensus rather than for majority control.
12. Trust the group. No one person is superior to the rest. The experience of all is richer than the experience of any one member. Work for consensus rather than majority control.

FACILITATING COMMENTS

The phrases below can help a meeting facilitator promote clear communication and ensure the purpose of the meeting is accomplished.

- Let's check that out with the rest of the group.
- Do you see it differently?
- How do you see the problem?
- Sounds like that's a problem we ought to address.
- I still don't have a handle on the real problem. What is it?
- What would *you* like to be doing?
- Oh, your perception is ... (describe). That's how you see the problem.
- Sounds like this is a real problem.
- Looks like you're really concerned about this issue.
- Feels like we're wasting valuable time. What would be a better use of our time?
- Sounds like you're all worn out.
- What are we doing right now?
- Say a little more about that.
- What's the purpose of this presentation?
- Hold on. I think we're talking about two problems, problem ______ and problem ______. I think they are both important, but let's talk about them one at a time.
- It's a big agenda today. Do you want to get through the whole agenda? (yes) Okay, if I push too hard, let me know.
- What do you want to have happen?
- Wait a second. We're jumping all around. We're brainstorming, discussing, clarifying, and debating. Let's stay in one phase at a time.
- That's an important consideration. Let's get that down. I'd like to come back to that after we finish the subject we're on, okay?

DEALING WITH PROBLEM MEMBERS

As leaders, we sometimes find ourselves working with a group whose members just don't interact well. It is helpful to pause and analyze what is happening. Is the problem one particular member? Two? More? The following are suggestions for dealing with a member who is keeping the group from being productive.

If a group member...	You might...
Talks endlessly and doesn't allow others to participate	Thank her or him for the input and suggest getting the views of others in the group. Politely point out that others need an opportunity to participate.
Must always present the negative side of an issue	Ask for group reactions to the expressed views or alternate solutions to the problem.
Talks about all subjects, whether they are pertinent or not	Call attention to the issue at hand, or suggest that because time is limited, you'll discuss the other issues later. In a nonjudgmental way, recommend getting back to the subject at hand.
Gets lost as he or she is trying to make a point	In a friendly manner, point out the digression. Draw attention to the discussion objectives and remind everyone that time is limited.
Distracts others by engaging in side conversations	Call on the talkers by name and either ask an easy question or restate the last opinion expressed by the group and ask their opinions. Try not to embarrass them.
Represents another group	Ask who she or he is speaking for and how your group can benefit from his or her participation in the discussion.
Acts superior to the group	Thank the person for his or her contributions and ask for other views on the issue.
States messages that are judgmental	Thank the member for his or her point of view, then ask the group for other sides of the issue that should be considered.
Is bored or indifferent	Try to draw him or her into the discussion by listing alternate solutions and asking for his or her opinion. Ask the person to lead a discussion.
Is timid or insecure	Draw out the person next to her/him, then ask her/his opinion of the view expressed.

TIPS FOR FACILITATING

Being a group facilitator can be different from being a group leader. Generally speaking, a facilitator takes an impartial and open approach to the group to help them meet their objectives. The American Youth Foundation (AYF) trains young leaders to be effective group facilitators in a number of their programs. AYF uses the acronym EASY to describe the job of a facilitator.

Elicit responses from each individual in the group. Every voice is important to the process and the facilitator should be alert to the entire group's membership to encourage full participation.

Ask open-ended questions to guide the group process. The facilitator recognizes when additional discussion is needed and formulates questions to provide this direction.

Summarize and re-state individual's ideas and opinions. This facet of the facilitator's job helps clarify each person's contribution to the group process and helps make sure that time isn't wasted on misinterpretation.

Your ideas and opinions are not shared. The facilitator must remain impartial and keep his or her ideas and reactions out of the group process. This requires self-discipline and trust that the group will undertake its responsibilities effectively.

WHAT TO WATCH OUT FOR IN MEETINGS...AND WHAT TO DO ABOUT IT!

NO CLEAR, AGREED UPON AGENDA (OR A MISUNDERSTOOD ONE)

At the start of the meeting, know the specific results you want to achieve by the end of the meeting. Either get together to plan the agenda, assign a person to phone around and then write the agenda, or develop one on the spot at the start of the meeting.

LEAVING THE PROCESS OF THE MEETING TO FATE

Separate the power (authority) and content (subject matter) from the process (how the meeting proceeds). As a meeting leader, either choose to facilitate yourself or ask a group member to do so.

NO DIRECTION

Ask. Where does this meeting fit in the overall plan for dealing with the issue? Take time for a planning process. Lay out the timeframe, steps, and interim deadlines. Go slow now to go fast later.

Mixing Purposes. Be clear (by using your agenda) about whether you're planning a procedure for dealing with a topic or actually dealing with it. In other words, you're either laying out the steps you'll take or actually taking a step. One purpose at a time.

Too many agenda items. An over-ambitious agenda is easy to fall into and sets the group up to fall short of its goals. Always ask: Are these goals realistic within the timeframe?

Shifting focus. Stay on the same subject; use the same process. For example, either brainstorm ideas or evaluate ideas, not both at the same time. List possible solutions or alternatives, then talk about criteria for selecting among them (time, cost, people required, likelihood of management support).

Lack of visual helpers. Find a way for participants to follow the subject as the meeting proceeds. Use flip charts or other means to help everyone focus on the content flow.

Unclear or incomplete action items or decisions to make. Pin down the who, what, where, and when on the spot. At the end of the meeting, check out all agreements made during the meeting.

Too many participants; the wrong participants; missing key people. When agendas have many items, more people need to be there even if they're only involved in one item.

Meeting dominated by one or two people. When this occurs, pull back and ask someone to facilitate. Don't miss the opportunity to make the most of your staff. Take the opportunity to participate yourself.

Lack of mutual understanding. Learn the issues facing other members. Explain your position. Ask members to repeat, in their own words, what they hear you saying. This will head off frustration and reluctance to cooperate.

Jumping in with a solution too early. There is a danger in arriving at a pet solution before clearly identifying or agreeing on the problem. Everyone should agree on the problem and the solution. Buy in ensures support.

Uneven preparation; varying levels of understanding. Set up a way for people to be prepared to talk about the issues at the same level of understanding.

Premature motions. Don't make a motion until the problem is adequately discussed and analyzed. If you can't agree on the problem, you probably can't agree on the solution (the motion). Premature motions divide the group and create artificial disagreements.

By Earl Reum
Adapted from *Meetings That Matter* (1993).

DANGER ZONES

Keep an eye out for these danger zones and try to avoid them throughout the year.

1. No preplanned agenda
2. Rushed planning
3. Lack of focus on one subject at a time
4. Too many items on the agenda
5. Meeting dominated by one or two people
6. Confused members
7. No encouragement to participate, summarize, or meet goals
8. Officers solving a problem before involving members.

Meeting management skills should include solutions to each of these problems.

Source: Dave Lilly, Oak Hill Elementary School, Lowell, Indiana (IASC)

ICEBREAKERS FOR MEETINGS

Q. Can you recommend some icebreakers for us to use at the beginning of our monthly meetings?

A: Icebreakers are an ideal way to use the first couple of minutes of a meeting to expand members' knowledge about each other and to add some fun. As you and the officers are planning agendas, try to build in time for a brief icebreaker from your library of icebreakers (that can begin with the ideas that follow). Having a folder of icebreakers handy also will be helpful if a meeting ends too quickly and you need to fill some time.

TWO TRUTHS AND A LIE

For this activity you will need to break into small groups of no more than 10 or 15 (otherwise people get bored waiting for their turn). You can suggest that people break up by the month they were born. Everyone takes a turn sharing two truths about themselves and one lie about themselves. The other members of the group have to guess which statement is the lie.

CIRCLE GAME

If you have a large space like a library or stage or large lobby area near your meeting room, you could play the Circle Game. Everyone takes a seat in a circle and one person stands in the middle and says, "I like people who... (have red hair)." The statement has to apply to the person standing in the middle. Then the center person and all the redheads (for example) move to another spot in the circle. Whoever is left without a seat becomes the person in the center. Have someone place a marker (piece of paper, book, etc.) for their standing spot in the center of the circle.

MYSTERY PERSON GAME

Have everyone split into three or four groups. Each person in the group writes down four things about themselves. Then the leader of the group reads the statements aloud and the other people try to guess whom the statements are about.

STAND UP AND SIT DOWN (Recommended for the first meeting of the year)

The leader makes a list of statements that might pertain to members of the group and reads each aloud. If the statement applies, the member stands up and then sits down. For example, "Stand up if you visited a college this summer," or "Stand up if you visited a beach." Try to develop enough questions so that everyone has an opportunity to stand up. About 20–25 questions is a good start.

ALPHABETICAL ORDER

Without talking, all members get in alphabetical order by first name. Do this at the first meeting with the new inductees and have the adviser or chapter president name all of those lined up. Many times the adviser will know the name (from the information form) but can't always connect to the face. This activity remedies that problem.

BINGO

Make a bingo board and put different objectives in the squares. Members get signatures of someone who has... taken an AP exam, drives a car, doesn't have a driver's license, plays a sport, has a job, has been accepted to a college, has a younger sibling, has an older sibling, etc. Prizes (candy) awarded to first one to get BINGO and the first one to fill the entire sheet.

QUICK QUIZ

Ask everyone to divide into groups of five or six and then hand out a quiz. For example,

Name the 50 United States: Give out a paper that lists the first letter of all the states. Members must fill in the rest.

Name the school staff: Hand out a sheet that tells how many teachers are in each department. The students write down their names.

Name that Christmas carol: Give out sheets with alternate names of Christmas carols. Students have to provide the real name. For example, petite male percussionist is Little Drummer Boy.

The top three or four teams get a bag of candy to share. Food is a great incentive!

MEETINGS AS TEAM-BUILDING EVENTS

Purpose: Individual needs, group needs, and task needs are all present during any group interaction.

Individual needs are felt the strongest in the beginning, and until they are met, the group never really moves on. It is important to take time at the beginning of the school year to build a team within your group.

Group needs are the needs that surface when an officer or member is aware of where the group is coming from and where the group is going, along with how the leaders fit into the scheme of things.

Task needs are the surface needs that bring the group together in the first place.

Investing time at the beginning of each meeting for a team-building activity will reap rewards in the long run.

Activities: The following team-building activities are designed to help members get to know one another and meet their needs.

1. *Forced selection.* Members of the group line up in the middle of the room. Members are asked to move to the right for one choice, and to the left for the other.

   Do you see yourself as:
   - A leader or a follower.
   - A Mercedes or a Jeep.
   - A rose or a wildflower.
   - A designer outfit or a pair of jeans.
   - A sunny day or a rainy day.

   Make up your own pairs from the many dichotomies that exist within the lives of your group members. Note: At the end of your exercise, notice the grouping of members—are there a significant bunch far to the left, middle, and right? They have things in common, so give them time to meet each other.

2. *Paired sharing.* Take turns sharing with a partner. Sit face-to-face. Practice effective listening when it is your partner's time to share.
   - Two things you like about yourself.
   - One talent you feel you have.
   - One of your "wins" in life.
   - A goal you plan to achieve.

4. *Ego boosting.* Go around the room and tell something positive about the person on your right.

5. *Involving members.* There are several ways to involve students in meetings. The following techniques are simple and are designed to introduce and relax the members.
   - Introduce each other after a few minutes of get-acquainted time.
   - Have self-introductions.
   - Identify one thing we do we'd like to do better.
   - Mix up seating arrangements.
   - Ask each other questions.
   - Wear different colored masks.
   - Create their own name tags.

   This list is just a beginning. Work with your officers to create more ideas to involve your students and enliven your meetings throughout the year.

By Earl Reum
Adapted from *Meetings That Matter* (1993).

EFFECTIVE AND MEANINGFUL MEETINGS: PROGRAM SUGGESTIONS

To help make your meetings more meaningful, consider adding a 5- to 15-minute program component to each meeting. These programs can be developed by you or one of your group leaders, or can utilize the talents and interests of staff members or community leaders.

Here are some suggested topics:

- Scholarships, Awards, Financial Aid
- Time Management Skills for Teens
- Organization Tips for School and for Life
- College Application Process
- Work Opportunities and Career Choices
- Service Opportunities in the Community
- Stress Management
- How to Prepare for Semester Exams
- How to Prepare for the SAT/ACT/PSAT or State Competency Exams
- Creativity Enhancement
- Leadership Roles in the Community
- Writing Essays for Applications and Awards
- Ethics
- Personal Resumes
- Summer Enhancement Opportunities

Run out of topics? Go to the source: your members!

Your guidance counselors, most of whom will welcome the opportunity to work with your members in a small group setting, can present many of these topics. In addition, if your group sponsors an annual service activity, learn more about the organization you support by asking a representative to present to your group. By developing a personal relationship with the recipient of the group's service, you'll prompt the members to be even more committed to service and success.

Don't forget to ask the school administration and the PTA for ideas or to present them with the opportunity to contribute regularly to your meetings. Their involvement will reassure your members of the importance of your group in the overall work of the school.

Finally, when your group attends state or national workshops and hears motivational stories or learns of new resources, have a delegate report back as his or her contribution to the program segment of your meetings. Similar contributions can be made by members who participate in other youth organizations, whether at school or in the community.

Program segments must be kept relatively short, but should be long enough to justify a visitor coming to your school for the presentation. Encourage presenters to provide handouts for members. Use media to enhance the presentation. Don't neglect the time as students are gathering and as they are leaving the meeting to support the day's program with music or relevant images.

Keep a file of your program ideas for your meetings—it will become an invaluable resource, and along with your files of icebreakers, will serve as a strong backup file to respond to meeting emergencies. Review and refresh your files each year and encourage your members to contribute. With a little work, you can build a strong new resource to help maintain your meetings as meaningful events.

Meeting Magic

By Mike Smith

In the first 30 seconds of your first meeting next semester, the attendees will decide what kind of a semester they are going to have. Regardless of the first semester's ups and downs, the second semester is an opportunity to make it better. Create a context for the emotional standards for your group's experience second semester—don't lose your message in a "same as last semester" opening. "Best semesters" do not just happen. They are built, painstakingly, one idea at a time. Make this first meeting—and all those the rest of the year—special with this check list:

Invitations. Yes, most of the people attending these meetings are required to be there but why not treat them as though they were not? What could it hurt? The idea is to make a "have to" into a "want to." Clearly stating the "desired outcome" of the meeting in the invitation promotes the desire to attend.

Agenda. This is a critical piece of the puzzle. The agenda should be:

- Action packed
- Time lined
- Information riddled
- Published in advance
- Adhered to.

Beginning and ending on time sets a professional tone and will help you get people to your next meeting. Nothing works better.

Location. If you hold your kickoff meeting in the same place it was last semester, then the "right brain message" is "Here we go again." Changing your location demonstrates your commitment to making the experience different.

Setting. Set the room to best accomplish the desired outcome of each agenda item: Use theater style for passing out information and praise (flow of emotion from one presenter to the entire group); use circles for sharing information among attendees (small circles can promote interaction which can easily be captured and shared with the entire group); or use a horseshoe to promote member interaction (this set up allows the members to see everyone in the group while their efforts are focused to the front).

In a perfect world there would be a large empty or tabled area for mixing and socializing before the meeting begins and a theater-style arrangement of chairs with a raised platform area for the speakers for the meeting itself.

Note: Moving your audience to a meeting setting sets a business tone.

Good sound system. To prevent side conversations and to maximize the benefits of the meeting, it is vital that each person be able to hear the presentations.

Food. In keeping with the "make it more friendly" idea, food is a must. Coffee (for adults) in the morning and juices, fruit, rolls, etc., at the break all add that special "we care" touch.

The food selection will influence the setup of the room. If you are providing food that requires forks or spoons, be sure you provide tables and chairs. Tables are good for the socializing time if you want social groups to re-form. However, if you want to mix the group better, provide only finger food and force them to stand and socialize.

Decorations. Use your marketing slogan and/or mission statement on banners. Use colorful tablecloths, plants, and centerpieces to make the room look different. There are people who love to decorate. The more people involved, the better. Decorations add that positive feeling to the gathering.

Music. Greeting attendees with good music clearly sends a friendly and professional message. Having it play as background to the registration or arrival process says a great deal about your meeting. Not having it says a lot as well. NOTE: As an attention-getting device to begin the meeting, turn the music up gradually for about two minutes, then, at the end of a selection, turn it off. The ensuing quiet often causes people to focus on those in charge.

First semester recap. Members enjoy reliving the successes of the first semester. Displaying photos, charts, and program results in the socializing area before the meeting begins provides members an opportunity to reminisce and reinforce the good things. It will help set the tone for the second semester. By using a display, you can shorten the "recap" portion of your program.

Nametags. Complain as they will about wearing nametags, not everyone knows everyone else. The typical human response to a room full of people whose names escape them is to develop a case of "shy." Large easily read first name nametags will promote better interaction among your participants.

Create a set of nametags that can be turned back in to be used at every meeting. Decorating them with colored ribbons or other symbols of service or honors makes them more valuable and gives members recognition for their accomplishments. One ribbon could be for years in the organization (different colors for each year increment). A second ribbon could be for special commendations such as officers, committee chairs, awards, or special effort you want to promote.

Special presentations. Honoring "one of us" is often like honoring "each of us," so sharing an honor of one of the attendees provides a good feeling to everyone. From professional recognition to successful accomplishments, family additions, or just a great vacation experience, any success can be shared. If nothing else, explain the meaning of the colored ribbons on the nametags so each member of a group can be proud and identify with others in that group.

Give-aways. Consider providing each attendee with a memento of the experience. This item could be anything to remind them of the positive feeling they had at the meeting. If you have a theme for the year, this is a great time to put it on pencils, calendars, magnets, mugs, and coasters—anything to tie the day together as you say good-bye!

Time. Everyone is too busy to waste time in meetings that go nowhere. Beginning and ending on time guarantees better attendance and more productivity. Doing it at this first meeting of the semester will send a great message.

As a precaution, design your agenda with a lead item that is not vital to everyone and acts as a buffer for emergency late arrivals. Establish the procedure for closing the door to the meeting to begin on time. This gesture protects the members from unwarranted interruptions. Open the door at each agenda item change to allow new arrivals to enter. They can catch up on what was done in their absence at the break or after the meeting. Once everyone understands the value of this procedure they will appreciate your efforts and will increase their efforts to arrive on time.

You never get a second chance to make a good first impression, but with the start of a new semester and attention to the details of your first meeting, you'll have a chance to make a better impression this time around.

Challenging Secrets for Successful Meetings

I have some secrets for you.

They seem almost stupid because they are so obvious. I know that you already know these things (along with secrets of your own).

But that is one of the secrets—you know things no one else knows. (And other people know things I don't know. That's one reason to conduct meetings.)

One of my secrets is that if you don't have planned meetings, you will have ineffective meetings. Unprepared members will try to discuss items that no one knew would be brought up. People will respond negatively. Confusion will create apathy, which will result in nonattendance, which can destroy your group.

Well-planned meetings give us positive direction to get things done, to tell people about what was accomplished and what is still being planned. They even tell us why people should be involved.

To have successful meetings, you need these elements:

Preparation. A room to help us reach goals, keep materials handy, space to reach out.

Planning. An agenda and time schedule that states objectives, shares ideas, involves those who attend, and gets us focused on action.

Purpose. Every meeting needs at least one goal and every member needs to know what those goals are. Members must feel involved in developing goals.

Processes. Interaction techniques, parliamentary procedure, brainstorming, and discussion group skills are needed in every meeting.

People. Everyone's opinion matters. Encourage, strengthen relations of group members, and value each person's ideas and opinions.

Conduct meetings with respect for each person. Move from gathering information to taking action. Encourage full participation of each person and each group within the group. Stay on task and on time. Clarify objectives. Create the arena for people to achieve and feel competent.

By Earl Reum

Adapted from *Meetings That Matter* (1993).

MEETINGS CHECKLIST

- ❑ Special invitation
- ❑ Agenda
- ❑ Changed location
- ❑ Good sound system
- ❑ Food
- ❑ Room arrangement
- ❑ Decorations
- ❑ Music
- ❑ First semester recap
- ❑ Nametags
- ❑ Special presentations
- ❑ Give-aways
- ❑ Begin and end on time

Follow-Up: Reporting and Evaluating

"When the only outcome of a meeting is to have another meeting, it has been a lousy meeting."
—President Herbert Hoover

The meeting is over. What's the proper follow-up? Various reporting procedures can expand the outreach of your meetings and assure the tasks developed by the meeting attendees are completed. And don't forget the importance of evaluation.

POSTMEETING CHECKLIST

Create a checklist for each function, leaving a column to designate who is responsible for completing each item and the date by which the tasks should be completed. Post the checklist for all to see. Public display will provide positive peer pressure for seeing that all jobs are completed in a timely manner. Suggested items to include are:

- Clean up the facility.
- Return equipment.
- Send thank-you notes to everyone who helped.
- Read and analyze meeting evaluation forms to see what could be done better next time.
- Prepare minutes of the meeting and distribute to everyone who attended.
- Phone or write to remind people of the commitments they made during the meeting: to complete jobs, contact people, carry out an activity, and so on.
- Make plans for the next meeting.

Keys to Successful Meetings: Did you find, after completing this checklist, that your original planning process did not include these postmeeting functions? Perhaps that is one feature that will emerge from your meeting evaluations.

DISTRIBUTING MEETING MINUTES

The responsibility for keeping an official record of what occurs at chapter meetings generally falls into the hands of the group secretary. The actual process of recording minutes can provide a deeper understanding of the issues your group faces, along with a clearer idea of what's important. The secretary should type minutes of the meetings as soon as possible after the meeting, while everything is still fresh in the mind. It's easy to forget details if you wait too long. Include the following items:

- Name of the group or committee
- Place, time, and date of the meeting
- Names of members present
- Names of members excused or absent
- Items discussed in the order listed on the agenda.

Briefly describe main points discussed and state actions taken such as votes, resolutions, and motions. If a member of the committee or chapter was assigned a task or volunteered for an assignment, clearly state the person's name and the responsibility accepted or assigned. It's a good idea to attach a separate sheet to the minutes that summarizes all action items for future reference. List each item on which action is needed and the responsible chapter member.

Proofread the minutes before submitting them and be sure to have the minutes approved by the president, committee chair, or adviser before distributing them to the members.

Once the minutes are created, proofed, approved, and printed, they need to be disseminated. You can do this in a variety of ways:

- E-mail a copy to all members of the group.
- Post the minutes on the group's Web site.
- Place copies in members' boxes in the group's office area.
- Post copies in every homeroom or classroom (of particular value for student councils and other student-body based organizations). For more focused groups, post a copy in relevant classrooms or in the faculty sponsor's classroom.
- With permission from the school secretary, make extra copies available in the main office and then announce their availability via a public address message or in the school newspaper.

Your goal should be to reach 100% of your group members.

SAMPLE MEETING AGENDA AND RECORD

FOR ____
Day   Date

Preparation is important; check these items well in advance:

Are we sure of a good program? ______________________________

Will our meeting place be ready and suitable for the program? ______________________________

Are committees ready to report? ______________________________

Have I checked the minutes of past meetings for deferred business? ______________________________

So we won't forget...Place any business deferred from this meeting on the agenda sheet for the next meeting and on the business and program schedule.

Do any of the programs planned for the next few weeks require that we set up committees now? ______________________________

Agenda

In the left-hand column, note the items to be handled

Record

After the item has been handled, write the action taken in the right-hand column to ensure that the item has not been sidetracked.

Who will preside? ______________________________

Theme: ______________________________

Flag ceremony by: ______________________________

Minutes of the last meeting: (only if essential)

Treasurer's report: ______________________________

Old business carried over from previous meetings (but not covered in pending committee reports):

ITEMS	ACTION TAKEN
1. ____________	1. ____________
2. ____________	2. ____________
3. ____________	3. ____________

Committee reports and actions on business deferred or assigned from the previous meetings:
Committee or individual: Report and action taken on it:

Committee or individual:	Report and action taken on it:
1. ____________	1. ____________
2. ____________	2. ____________
3. ____________	3. ____________

New business and committee reports concerned with these items. (Refer all new items that are not ready for proper consideration now to a regular or special committee to get the facts, study them, and make recommendations.)

Item	Action—or Referred to
1. ____________________	1. ____________________
2. ____________________	2. ____________________
3. ____________________	3. ____________________
4. ____________________	4. ____________________

Other committee reports and announcements that require no action:

1. ______________________________
2. ______________________________
3. ______________________________
4. ______________________________

Committees appointed and tasks assigned:
(Note now, on the proper meeting agenda page, when these committees are to report.)

Program (Note here any special program-related information. After the meeting, make a brief record of the who, what, where, and why of this meeting to help with recalling essential information at a later date.)

Closing (how): ______________________________
Completed by: ____________________ Date: ____________________
Reviewed/Approved by (adviser): ______________________________

REPORTING CHECKLIST

Whatever method you use for reporting out from your meetings, consider the following questions about the effectiveness of your reporting.

1. **Timing.** Are your reports distributed in a timely manner? Are you using the most efficient method for getting the word out to your group members?

2. **Quality.** Is the content well-written and understandable by the members of our group? If too many corrections or too many questions arise at a meeting when the minutes are reviewed, this could be a sign that your recordkeeper needs a little training or assistance.

3. **Distribution.** Did all members receive copies after the meeting? To keep every member engaged in your group activities, it is essential to keep every member well-informed of the events from your meetings. Who else needs to know? Does the principal have a copy of your reports to keep her up-to-date about your group activities? Do faculty members need access to this information? Are there details that should be shared with the superintendent or school board? (Check with the adviser and principal before initiating this contact.)

4. **Archives.** Have copies of the minutes and reports--both hard copy and electronic--been filed in the group files for future reference? Do your group leaders have quick access to these files?

EVALUATING YOUR MEETINGS

Evaluating and responding to the results of the evaluations are the final steps in the Plan/Do/Follow-up model for meetings. Here are a variety of tools to help you evaluate the effectiveness of your meetings.

MEETING EVALUATION FORM

Instructions. Think about the meeting you just attended. Check the statements below that most accurately describe your observations.

1. **Direction**
   a. Comments slid from point to point; people didn't seem to really care about what they were saying.
   b. There was harmonious discussion among agreeable people.
   c. One person or several took over and controlled the topic and the flow of discussion.
   d. The leader stepped in to try to keep the session organized, on track, and on time.
   e. There was a lively exchange of views; each person regulated his or her own contributions.

2. **Decision Making**
   a. Remarks were not picked up; they fell like lead balloons.
   b. After support of a thought by one or two, the course of action developed.
   c. One or a few people bulldozed the process.
   d. Compromise was the key to decisions.
   e. Decisions were based on complete understanding and agreement.

3. **Expressing Ideas**
   a. Ideas and opinions were expressed with little conviction.
   b. Polite give-and-take resulted in a friendly session.
   c. Discussions were on a "win your own point" basis; people held tight to their views.
   d. Although different ideas and opinions were expressed, acceptable positions were reached; people moved from their positions to make group progress.
   e. Ideas and convictions were expressed frankly and honestly; differences were worked through to mutual understanding.

4. **Atmosphere**
   a. Going through the paces; flat, lifeless.
   b. Easygoing and pleasant.
   c. Win-lose competitiveness; critical and tense.
   d. Interesting and satisfying.
   e. Penetrating and rewarding, challenging, caring.

5. **Evaluation**
   a. Little or no attention given to discussing group action.
   b. Compliments given, but faults not examined.
   c Fault-finding; non-constructive criticism.
   d. Suggestions of how to do differently or better.
   e. Real effort to evaluate the group while it was working, both for improving action and for learning.

POSTMEETING REACTIONS FORM: PERSONAL EVALUATION

Directions: Rank in order each statement in each set on a scale of 1 (most like) to 10 (least like) to describe the meeting and your behavior. In each set, first identify the statement you would rank 1, then the one you would rank 10, then 2, then 9—alternating toward the middle of the scale.

The meeting progressed like this:

______ There was much warmth and friendliness.

______ There was much aggressive behavior.

______ People were uninterested and uninvolved.

______ We were in need of help.

______ Much of the conversation was irrelevant.

______ We were strictly task-oriented.

______ The members were very polite.

______ There was much underlying irritation.

______ We worked on our process issues.

______ Officers were organized and well-prepared.

My behavior was like this:

______ I was warm and friendly to some.

______ I did not participate much.

______ I concentrated on the job.

______ I tried to get everyone involved.

______ I took over the leadership.

______ I was polite to all.

______ My suggestions were frequently off the point.

______ I was a follower.

______ I was irritated.

______ I was eager and aggressive.

GROUP EVALUATION SHEET

A. Evaluate your group on the following scales by rating each item from 1 to 10 (10 being ideal).

Listening

1. People talked past each other with few genuine attempts to understand others.

   Careful listening to others' views.

   1 2 3 4 5 6 7 8 9 10

Openness

2. Discussion was polite, cautious; views held little conviction.

   Ideas expressed with candor, differences.

   1 2 3 4 5 6 7 8 9 10

Task-Orientation

3. Discussion was disorganized and rambled from point to point.

   Discussion stayed on track to get the task accomplished.

   1 2 3 4 5 6 7 8 9 10

Participation

4. Discussion was dominated by a few.

   There was lively interplay; many members contributed without domination.

   1 2 3 4 5 6 7 8 9 10

Atmosphere

5. The atmosphere of the meeting was tense, strained, somewhat unpleasant, and flat.

   The atmosphere was satisfying, challenging, and stimulating.

   1 2 3 4 5 6 7 8 9 10

Mutual Support

6. Every person was out for her- or himself. Members had genuine concern for each other.

   1 2 3 4 5 6 7 8 9 10

B. How would you describe the sense of leadership in the group?

C. How well were the meeting tasks accomplished?

GIVING AND RECEIVING FEEDBACK

Evaluation always generates feedback to and from everyone involved in your meetings. A number of guidelines can help make giving and receiving feedback more valuable. Keep in mind that these are guidelines, not rules, so they are not set in stone.

Guidelines for Giving Feedback

1. **Good timing**—The sooner the feedback is given, the better. When feedback is immediate, the receiver is likely to be able to link the feedback to the actual event and may still feel the emotions he or she felt during the meeting. Give feedback only when it's clear that the receiver is ready for it. If the receiver is distracted, he or she may not pay attention or may misinterpret what you say. Feedback should be given when it's more likely to be helpful than harmful. Feedback is not helpful if the receiver believes other work demands more attention at that time or if you give negative feedback in front of others.
2. **Descriptive not interpretive**—Feedback should be a clear report of the facts, not your ideas about why things happened or what they meant. It is up to the receiver to invite your interpretation.
3. **Something new**—Don't state the obvious. Consider whether your observations are something that the receiver truly may not have been aware of. Many times, the most helpful information is not simply a report of what you saw the receiver doing, but rather the way it caused you to feel or the situation you felt it put you in.
4. **It's changeable**—Feedback can lead to improvements only when it is about things that can be changed. However, giving feedback should not be confused with asking a person to change. You might include in your feedback some suggestions for change, but it's the receiver's responsibility to decide what to do with the feedback you provide.
5. **Not an overload**—It can be easy to just start ticking off a long list of points you want to make. Instead, share only the points that are most important to the helping the other person reach his or her goals.
6. **Be helpful**—Always consider your own reasons for giving your reactions. Are you trying to help the receiver or are you really trying to get the receiver to do something that would help you? If you are doing more than trying to help the receiver, you should share your additional reasons so he or she will better understand what you are saying.
7. **Giver shares something**—Giving feedback can sometimes create a "one-upsmanship" climate. The receiver goes away feeling as though he or she is "not as good" as the evaluator. The exchange can be more positive and productive if it's more of a dialogue than a lecture.

Guidelines for Receiving Feedback

Be specific—Let the evaluator know what specific areas you'd like to focus on with regard to feedback and reactions.

Check what you have heard—Check to be sure you understand what the evaluator is trying to say.

Share your reactions—Let your evaluator know what you think about his or her feedback. Did it help you? How could it have been more helpful?

By Earl Reum

Adapted from *Meetings That Matter* (1993).

MEETING EVALUATION FORM

Instructions: Circle the appropriate number following each description: Five = always; four = nearly always; three = sometimes; two = not very often; one = almost never. Total your score at the end in the space provided.

1. Each regular meeting is scheduled well in advance with the time posted.
   5 4 3 2 1
2. The executive committee meets before each meeting.
   5 4 3 2 1
3. Members attend all meetings regularly.
   5 4 3 2 1
4. The meetings always start and close on time.
   5 4 3 2 1
5. The meetings are fun.
   5 4 3 2 1
6. The adviser does not have to tell everyone what to do.
   5 4 3 2 1
7. The meetings are orderly with correct parliamentary procedure being used.
   5 4 3 2 1
8. An agenda of the meeting is posted well in advance of each meeting or a copy is given to each member prior to meetings.
   5 4 3 2 1
9. All the officers know their roles and responsibilities regarding the conduct of meetings.
   5 4 3 2 1
10. The meetings are not run by a small group of members; everyone participates.
    5 4 3 2 1
11. The meetings accomplish what they are supposed to accomplish.
    5 4 3 2 1
12. The organization does not have to call special meetings very often.
    5 4 3 2 1
13. There is no "horse play" or "goofing around" during meetings.
    5 4 3 2 1
14. Committee reports and officer reports are given regularly and effectively.
    5 4 3 2 1
15. Nonmembers who are invited to attend the meetings are impressed by what they see.
    5 4 3 2 1
16. Members are allowed to express their points of view.
    5 4 3 2 1
17. The meetings do not drag out over a long period of time.
    5 4 3 2 1
18. The meetings never seem cut-and-dried.
    5 4 3 2 1

Total: ____________

A LEADERS' ANALYSIS OF COMMON MEETING PROBLEMS

Problems with: And what do I do about them:*

Process
- People try to do lots of jobs simultaneously
- Confusion between process and content
- Personal attacks on people, the organization, the process, or the plan

Roles
- Unclear roles and responsibilities
- Manipulation of people or people's jobs
- Hidden agendas

Information Handling
- Data overload
- Repetition and wheel spinning

Decision-Making
- Win/lose approaches
- Power and authority issues

Environment
- Too hot, too cold, too noisy, too formal
- Poor seating arrangements

Preparation And Follow Up
- Confused objectives and expectations
- Lack of planning
- No action

*You may want to add additional problem areas under each of these topics based on local meeting experience.

Key to Success: When working on your meetings as a topic for your local leadership workshop, assign each of these topics to a small group and have each group write or act out a skit portraying these problems. Ask the audience to discuss the problem portrayed and suggest ways of effectively handling such situations during the year. Write out the scripts or videotape the presentations to serve as review during the year or to share with other organizations on campus.

Special Notes for Advisers

"I sit in on pitchers' meetings every once in a while."
—Barry Bonds, San Francisco Giants

The responsibility for teaching students proper meeting management skills often falls into the hands of the activity adviser. Let's explore some important aspects of the adviser's role in managing meetings and in training students to be effective meeting planners and managers.

THE ACTIVITIES ADVISER AS MEETING MANAGER

Let the students plan, carry out, and evaluate, but advisers must assume the role of supervisor or manager of the process. Here are some of the qualities of effective meeting managers.

- Serves as a role model
- Lets students perform in the arena
- Prepares people before the action
- Motivates before, during, after
- Is a team builder
- Picks up the pieces
- Understands and uses many different ways for learning
- Manages each student leader's skills for the benefit of the team
- Determines the game plan based on the talents of the students
- Works on strengths and weaknesses of participants
- Develops students to be independent
- Helps people succeed appropriate to their level
- Respects each group member
- Cares significantly and deeply
- Extracts the positive from members, even in failure situations
- Empowers members with skills development and helps them learn

- Maintains perspective—keeps the big picture in mind
- Is authentic
- Teaches discipline
- Creates a sense of family
- Is personally healthy and energetic
- Is an advocate for students
- Provides success at incremental steps
- Challenges students
- Is creative and resourceful
- Teaches with experiential situations
- Does not personally have to own the abilities being taught.

Meetings will be more effective when we guide students through them.

MEETING SKILLS: GROUP PROCESS OBJECTIVES FOR AN ADVISER

We need to provide students with an awareness of the differences between content and process. There is more to groups than just solving problems or doing projects. We need to help develop student skills in group process on three levels: sensitivity, diagnostic ability, and action skills.

For example:

Sensitivity—Do I notice that person X seems distracted? Do I notice how the rest of the group reacts?

Diagnostic Ability—Do I understand why person X does not participate? Is it a case of the group's goal not being clear? Is it a communication problem, an organizational one?

Action Skill—Can I actually step in and help the group by bringing in the needed function effectively? If I have noticed that person X is distracted and decided that the probable trouble is that the group is not actively involved in the topic at hand and will permit and encourage divergence, then there is still the problem of action. What can I do or say to help the group?

We need to provide development and practice in these skills:

- Testing for the presence of group consensus at a given point
- Supporting other group members
- Recognizing the causes of types of disruptive behaviors and how to deal with them
- Identifying what functional roles students assume in group situations where they are the leader, a participant, a newcomer, etc.

We also need to make clear some of the differences among meeting skills and work with groups to use these various skills.

- Awareness of process/product—kind of meeting
- Effect of knowing the other group members and how they behave
- The safety of the setting to try out alternative styles and strategies to various group members

We need to explore how a group exerts pressure on its members to conform and the implications of such activity.

By Earl Reum
Adapted from *Meetings That Matter* (1993).

PROCESSING: A LEARNING EXPERIENCE

As with all projects and events we undertake with student leaders, we must process the activity with them to generate group and personal growth and learning. Use the following list of suggested questions as a guide to processing the impact of your meetings.

FIRST: EXPERIENCE

NEXT: DESCRIBE (ADJECTIVES/OBJECTIVE TRUTHS)

- Describe what happened and the sequence of events. What was going on? Be specific with details.
- Who else had the same experience? Saw what I saw? Felt the same way?
- Who reacted the same? Differently?
- What was my personal reaction?
- How did I internalize these events?
- How do I feel different now?
- How did I feel different then?
- What true feelings connect with this event?
- Which of my feelings conflicted with fact at the time? Now?

NOW: INTERPRET (MAKING SENSE OF DATA)

- How do I account for what happened?
- What does it truly mean to me?
- How was it good, bad, indifferent?
- What do I better understand about myself, my group, my goals, the process? Why?

NEXT: FORMULATE TRUTHS (DRAWING CONNECTIONS)

- What does all of this suggest to me?
  In general:
  Specifically:
- What universal principles do I see operating here?
- How do these events relate to other experiences of my life?
- What things, events, ideas do I associate with all this?
- What did I learn—relearn?
- What hopes were stirred for me?

APPLY TO THE NEXT TIME (TO USE IN FUTURE SITUATIONS)

- How can I apply or transfer these truths, experiences, events, feelings?
- What could I do to hold onto what is important here?
- What am I going to do in my life to use these experiences?
- What are the consequences of doing/not doing what I have chosen to do?
- What changes can I make which will achieve these ideas and goals?
- What would I do differently? What the same?
- What life-support systems were created/refurbished here? How? Why? When?
- What really happened?
- What did I see?
- What are the facts?
- Who says so?

- Where is it reported? How?
- What did I hear?
- What is most real about all this?
- What other feelings do I have about these events?
- What is the sequence?
- How can I learn to describe this better?
- What did I learn?
- What surprised me?
- What surprised others?
- What was funny? Why?
- Was I offended or edified?
- Was I hurt? Angry? Confused? Hopeful? Discouraged?
- How can I keep an attitude of positive expectation?

ROLE FUNCTIONS IN A GROUP

TASK ROLES: REQUIRED TO SELECT AND CARRY OUT GROUP ACTIVITIES

1. **Initiating activity.** Proposing solutions, suggesting new ideas, new definitions of the problem, new approaches to the problem, or new organization of strategies.
2. **Seeking information.** Asking for clarification of suggestions, requesting additional information or facts or opinion of experts.
3. **Seeking opinions.** Looking for an expression of feeling about something from the members, seeking clarification of values, suggestions, or ideas.
4. **Giving information.** Offering facts or generalizations; relating one's own experience to the group problem to illustrate ideas.
5. **Giving opinions.** Stating an opinion or belief concerning a suggestion or one of several suggestions, particularly concerning its value rather than its factual basis.
6. **Elaborating.** Clarifying, giving examples or developing meanings, trying to envision how a proposal might work if adopted.
7. **Coordinating.** Showing relationships among various ideas or suggestions, trying to pull ideas and suggestions together, trying to draw together activities of various subgroups or members.
8. **Summarizing.** Pulling together related ideas or suggestions, restating suggestions after the group has discussed them.

GROUP-BUILDING ROLES: REQUIRED TO STRENGTHEN THE GROUP

1. **Encouraging.** Being friendly, warm, and responsive to others; praising others and their ideas; agreeing with and accepting contributions of others.
2. **Gatekeeping.** Encouraging a quiet member contribute to the group or suggesting limited talking time for everyone so that each will have a chance to be heard.
3. **Setting standards.** Setting standards for the group with regard to content, procedures, or decisions; reminding the group to avoid decisions that conflict with group standards.
4. **Following.** Supporting the decisions of the group; thoughtfully accepting ideas of others; and serving as respectful audience during group discussions.

5. **Expressing group feelings.** Summarizing the general feeling of the group and describing reactions of the group to ideas or solutions.

GROUP MAINTENANCE ROLES: REQUIRED TO MAINTAIN GROUP HEALTH

1. **Evaluating.** Comparing group decisions or accomplishments with group standards; measuring accomplishments against goals.
2. **Diagnosing.** Identifying problems and selecting appropriate steps to allow progress.
3. **Testing for consensus.** Asking for group opinions to find out whether the group is nearing consensus on a decision; sending up trial balloons to test group opinions.
4. **Mediating.** Harmonizing; proposing compromise solutions.
5. **Relieving tension.** Draining negative feeling by injecting humor or calming troubled waters; viewing a tense situation in a wider context.

From time to time, people behave in ways that actually harm the group and the work it is trying to do. Some of the more common types of negative behaviors are described below.

TYPES OF NEGATIVE BEHAVIOR

1. **Bullying.** Working for status by criticizing or blaming others; displaying hostility against the group or an individual; deflating the ego or status of others.
2. **Blocking.** Interfering with the progress of the group by going off on a tangent; citing personal experiences unrelated to the problem; arguing too much on a point, rejecting ideas without consideration.
3. **Self-confessing.** Using the group as a sounding board; expressing personal, nongroup-oriented feelings or points of view.
4. **Competing.** Vying with others to produce the best idea, talk the most, play the most roles, gain favor with the leader.
5. **Seeking sympathy.** Trying to encourage other group members to be sympathetic to one's problems or misfortunes; deploring one's own situation or disparaging one's own ideas to gain support.
6. **Special pleading.** Introducing or supporting suggestions related to one's own pet concerns or philosophies; lobbying.
7. **Horsing around.** Clowning, joking, mimicking, disrupting the work of the group.
8. **Seeking recognition.** Attempting to call attention to one's self by loud or excessive talking, extreme ideas, unusual behavior.
9. **Withdrawal.** Acting indifferent or passive; resorting to excessive formality, day dreaming, doodling, whispering to others, wandering from the subject, distracting.

Guard against the tendency to blame any person who falls into negative behavior. It is more useful to regard such behavior as a symptom that all is not well with the group's ability to satisfy individual needs through group-centered activity. People need to be alert to the fact that each person is likely to interpret such behaviors differently. Additional resources for understanding group process can be found in Chapter 7.

LOCAL STUDENT LEADERSHIP TRAINING

Meeting management and meeting skills do not always come naturally. Training for these skill sets can be a valuable element of any student activity on campus. Many high schools and middle level schools face the problem in the democratic handling of student councils, clubs, and other activities of students who are elected to office but have little knowledge or ability in the field of leadership and meeting management. It may be the sports team captain who is elected president of the student council after leading the team to a championship. It may be the "glamour girl" who is elected to office after winning Homecoming Queen. It may be the top student in the class who excels in classroom performance but who has never been given the opportunity to lead. Or it may be the average student who is elected among an average group of candidates.

Any or all of these students may find themselves tongue-tied and embarrassed, feeling inadequate when they must assume the duties of their elected offices. A minority of students may be "natural born" leaders, but the majority must learn how.

This problem can be handled by an annual leadership training program for officers and potential officers. Held before annual elections (whether fall or spring), these workshops can help prepare a variety of students for leadership roles in various aspects of school life. All clubs and organizations on campus can be invited to participate. Students who have an interest in assuming a leadership role can be encouraged to sign up as well.

It is important to first identify and look at the goals of any such training activity. Some suggested goals are:

1. To improve student leadership efforts in running meetings
2. To learn how to engage all members of the club/organization in meetings
3. To review the specific duties of office for standard officers in a group
4. To reinforce the role that student leaders play in student activities on campus, and the role models that they serve as.

Other goals can be developed by those responsible for planning and implementing the program.

With approval and support of the principal, several faculty advisers or even experts from outside the school can plan and lead the sessions. Most helpful will be those sessions led by current student leaders who have already undergone the training. The following model consists of three one-period (hour) meetings with a formal list of students having been invited to attend. Specific resources for use during each of these sessions will be included at the end. Local guidelines will determine whether students can be excused from class to participate in this type of training or whether it will need to be held outside of classroom hours. (An alternative is to conduct these sessions as a one-day training on a Saturday, or to incorporate them into a weekend retreat for student leaders sponsored by the school.)

Let's review some suggested content for the three sessions:

Session 1: The first session includes discussion and activities on the qualities and responsibilities of leadership. After training goals are reviewed and participants are allowed to introduce themselves (brief icebreakers or mixers are encouraged), such leadership traits as positive attitude, trustworthiness, responsibility, open-mindedness, initiative and school spirit can be reviewed.

Personality types can be explored using programs such as True Colors (www.truecolors.org). Identifying what principals, faculty members, parents, and of course the student body look for in student leaders sets the stage for the skills to be taught. Participants are encouraged to create personal reflections on the content of this session and to be prepared to share some of their observations at the next meeting.

Session 2: The second session can focus on methods and techniques of discussion and planning. A review of various types of meetings that each student leader will need to facilitate and the best format to use for various functions are covered. Aspects of the planning process needed to assure a successful outcome should be reviewed, along with ways to evaluate the success of the meetings that are held are also important.

Session 3: The third session zeroes in on meeting management skills. A review of a standard agenda, duties of office for traditional officers, along with procedures for motions, minutes, and discussion should be reviewed. A sample meeting skit, delineating the traditional language for presiding and contributing officers is helpful to review. A concluding portion of this session can sort students out according to the various groups they represent and have them identify the various meetings and projects they will be undertaking for the school year, identifying the meeting style most suitable for each function. Finally, student participants should each receive a signed certificate upon completion of all three sessions in recognition of their successful training experience.

To facilitate ongoing reference to the content of this training, organizers can create a notebook for each participant containing the essential resources discussed. This leadership notebook can be reviewed and updated each year as new information is brought to the school from conferences and workshops during the year. In addition, copies of the content presented at the workshop and the notebooks should be shared with the faculty advisers of each group represented in the training.

This training model presents schools with a simple and effective structure for addressing the training of student leaders in student activities on campus. Content can be adapted to be age appropriate (e.g., high school or middle level) and to reflect the structure and guidelines for student activities that exist locally. Having all officers participate simultaneously, as opposed to each group undertaking its own independent training, brings forth some consistency in student leadership skills. Providing this as an annual training opportunity develops continuity in the quality of student programs on campus from one year to the next. Maintaining this training as a priority in the minds of the administrators and faculty will assure ongoing support for student activities throughout the years.

Adapted from How We Do It articles originally published in *Student Activities*, January 1958, as implemented by Wantagh (NY) High School; Stevens & Wright (1992) *Leadership Retreats*, and Reum (1999), *Organizing an Inter-Club Leadership Conference*.

MANAGING MEETINGS FOR STUDENT GROUPS

Managing meetings is very different from what we usually think of as teaching. We judgmentally evaluate, correct, grade, and assess student response and performance. But student meetings require a relationship of acceptance and support—an atmosphere of honesty, openness, mutual discovery... even excitement.

Managing meetings means encouraging and guiding with the agreement and trust of the student leaders involved. We discover that we are on the same team, needing skills, and working together for common purposes. Activity advisers help students develop leadership knowledge, habits, and skills—and then free students to use these for the benefit of civilization.

It is ideal to have the executive committee develop the agenda without our being involved except as another member of the group, contributing items, mentioning possibilities, preparing these leaders for possible eventualities at the meeting. The leadership team can set the goals for the meeting without our help. It is enormously difficult to keep our mouths shut. Our urge is to moralize, to lecture. Great advisers focus on helping student leaders discover who they are, where they're going, and the best way to get there.

Managing/advising nurtures the self-discovery, self-direction, and self-enhancement process. Leaders will discover their incredible power eventually, but we need to support their sense of confidence and self-worth with reminder capsules that clue them into choosing appropriate meeting skills at the time they are needed.

We must focus on a role that relates to students in a respectful, non-judgmental, even trusting manner that allows students to explore, discover, set goals, and make commitments to objectives they have envisioned for themselves.

The truly effective adviser will focus on the change of behavior within a student that allows a greater success in the arena. We must be certain that the worth of the student is never in question, nor the potential and capability. Responsibility for change is with the student, not the teacher. Change will occur in the context of acceptance and trust. People feel free to move in brand new directions when they don't have to defend themselves, or feel a need to resist someone else who is trying to change them.

People tend to change when they have meaningfully participated in the decision to change. People tend to support a change that they personally help design; they tend to resist changes they do not help design. (They can be vocally critical as well.)

Individuals tend to change when they are convinced that the rewards for change exceed the pains of change. People tend to change when they see others changing—particularly when the direction of change is supported by valued people.

Individuals and groups tend to change more readily in situations without threat or judgment. People tend to change when they personally have (or can acquire) the competencies, knowledge, and skills required by the change.

Individuals tend to change to the degree they trust the motives of the adviser who is attempting to make the change. People will change more readily if they are able to influence the adviser who is attempting to influence them.

Individuals and groups tend to change to the degree that they see the change as "successful" (especially if they are able to gather the information for themselves). People tend to maintain change to the extent that change is supported by their environment. They resist change when "the system" resists it. Peer pressure is a "heavy system"!

MANAGING MEETINGS FOR STUDENT GROUPS (cont.)

Student leaders can develop the necessary skills to create a climate that supports change—in the meeting. Individuals tend to maintain change if there is a public commitment to the change, or if the whole team supports the direction and idea of the change.

People tend to resist change to the degree that they feel it is imposed upon them. A sense of free choice is essential for people to build a team. It is tempting, fun, and very easy to suggest change for others. Don't do it.

It is difficult and requires courage, persistence, faith, and good humor to change oneself, and every day great advisers do that. Search out skills, strengths, the emphasis, a strategy, a plan for win-win, total commitment to the good of the group. We do that when we empower each student leader by encouraging appropriate meeting skills.

We truly need to move leaders from an ego focus to identification with their real selves. The experience of self is a recognition of personal uniqueness and universality. We discover that everyone is terrified, that my experiences are your experiences, and we can share that. We connect our leaders with the infinite, a oneness of spirit from which will emerge love, compassion, awareness, and committed action.

Responsibility will begin for young people as an awareness of need, of belonging, of loneliness, and of universal discovery in an environment without judgment, which most of our teaching experiences have given us. We must commonly discover that we are each personally responsible for our own behavior, our choices, our lives.

Meeting responsibilities become powerful human support systems, not dull burdens. Satisfaction and success will come as each meeting happens; we review the evaluations, and discover the responsibilities pay off. Our search for truth will be the daily experiencing of it in the actual arena of working with others—with myself at the sideline, watching a student utilize the skills which we have mutually nourished for the purpose of this meeting, this day, in this school.

See Chapter 7 for other helpful activities to assist you in running a local leadership workshop.

By Earl Reum

Adapted from *Meetings That Matter* (1993).

Additional Resources: Tools for Better Meeting Management

■

"Successful meetings (business, general, or otherwise) require good planning and a clear agenda. This, in turn, requires strong leadership."
—Irene Doo, educator

This chapter offers some additional resources to help make your meetings more effective:

7.1 AGENDAS

MANAGEMENT TOOL: SAMPLE MEETING AGENDA

As you plan meetings for your group, consider using the model below as a template for your meeting agenda. Always have a written agenda and distribute it prior to the meeting so that your members know 1) what their responsibilities are if they appear on the agenda, and 2) what topics will be discussed at the meeting so that they can prepare their thoughts on the issues ahead of time. Officers, particularly the president, are encouraged to work with the adviser to prepare each meeting's agenda. Care should be given to consult the agendas and minutes from previous meetings to determine those issues that merit continued consideration.

Prior to the meeting:

- A copy of the agenda is distributed to all members or made available for viewing.
- A presiding officer for the meeting is identified and time taken with this individual to review the agenda items.
- Individuals with specific responsibilities at the upcoming meeting (e.g., secretary, treasurer, committee chairs, project chairs, etc.) are notified about the nature of their duties for the meeting and when they appear on the agenda.
- Members are notified and reminded of the meeting time and place.

SAMPLE AGENDA OUTLINE

I. Call to Order (Pledge of Allegiance or other pledge can be added)

II. Roll Call/Attendance

III. Minutes of the Previous Meeting (review and approval)

IV. Treasurer's Report* (review and approval)

V. Committee Reports*

   A. Standing Committee reports

   B. Special Committee reports

VI. Old/Unfinished Business**: Carried over from the last or previous meetings

VII. New Business**

VIII. Other Reports, Announcements and Reminders of Events or Responsibilities, including but not limited to the announcement of the date and time of the next regularly scheduled meeting of this group.

IX. Program: Guest presentation or program topic for this meeting (location of this segment of the meeting agenda may depend on the nature of the content and the scheduling needs of the guest presenter, e.g. the principal who may need to speak at the beginning of the meeting instead of the end).

X. Adjournment

* It is recommended that all reports be submitted in writing to the secretary by the end of the meeting, and that a time limit and/or format be given to each report-giver to assure consistent and informative reporting.

** In sections VI. and VII. above, Old and New Business, when motions are presented for consideration by the membership, it is strongly recommended that the group utilize the fundamental principles of meeting management from *Robert's Rules of Order* or other established systems of meeting management to consider each topic.

AGENDA-PLANNING EXERCISE

Scene: It is Thursday, November 4, a meeting after school of your group's Executive Committee. Your mission is to prepare the agenda for next week's group meeting.

Facts to Consider: Your meeting will take place Wednesday, November 10 at 3 p.m. in the school library. All officers, the adviser, committee chairpersons, and members will be expected to attend. When determining the order of events, it is acceptable to utilize alphabetical and/or chronological order of events or groups when working with multiple events in a single category.

Instructions: Using the recommended agenda format above as a guide, consider the following items for inclusion on the agenda. Number each of the items (1 to 13) to indicate the proper order in which they should appear on the meeting day.

The president will report on the volunteers who assisted with decorations at the Homecoming Dance on October 22.

At the last monthly meeting, held October 13, members asked for a report on the tutoring program schedule for the group this year. A response has been prepared by the president and the adviser for presentation.

The Service Project Committee, a standing committee of your group, would like to provide the plans for the group's annual Food Drive, currently scheduled for the week before Thanksgiving.

The president will report on responses to member questions raised at last month's meeting and answered by the principal, Ms. Felder, at the regular monthly meeting with the principal held on October 28.

Announcement of the date and location of the December meeting.

The president wishes to ask the secretary to go to a party next Saturday night at the head cheerleader's house.

The principal has sent the president and adviser a note requesting that she be given 5 minutes to address the group in order to respond to plans for second semester group activities.

The Special Committee on assisting the neighboring middle school has a report to make on their current plans.

The formal adjournment of the meeting.

The Fund-Raising Committee, a standing committee of the group, has finished its plans for the spring fundraiser and wishes to report.

The adviser, Mr. Marano, has an announcement to make regarding the member selection procedures schedule for the spring.

The SADD chapter, whose president is a member of your group, has a new request to make to help promote "SADD Week" this spring by co-sponsoring an assembly for the student body.

The vice-president wishes to correct the minutes of the last meeting with the correct dates for second semester activities, misprinted in the recently distributed set of minutes.

7.2 WORKING IN GROUPS: GROUP PROCESS 101

The heart of an effective student group is the ability to build a warm, open relationship with each person you serve. In politics, this person is generally referred to as "John Q. Public." In sales, this person is the "consumer." In psychology, the person is referred to as the "client," and in student government, this person is every person that is a part of your school!

Your effectiveness as a student leader depends on how well you function with people in groups, such as your peers, the faculty, the administration, and all the support personnel of your school. Your ability not only to build warm, open relationships, but to help make rules of group interaction explicit and to play a variety of responsible roles in the group related to its effectiveness will help determine whether or not you and your fellow group members feel a sense of mutual trust, responsibility, and freedom to grow.

The way you relate to others, whether it's one-to-one or in groups, reflects how you feel about your own worth and the worth of others. Attitudes are difficult to measure directly. In the long run, only you will know whether your attitudes toward those you serve reflect the basic philosophy about the worth of each individual, about self-reliance, and the concept of a demonstrated professionalism in your leadership skills.

All of us are involved in group process situations. Some are informal—such as with relatives or friends. Others are more formalized situations with specific responsibilities and directions. It is important to remember that within every group there are people with needs and wants. Some members are take-charge people and others are task oriented. Basically, leadership is executing a particular role within an organized group, and this role is defined essentially in terms of power or the ability to influence others. A leader in one group may not emerge as the leader in another group. As membership changes, the leader may change, or, if the purpose or activities change, the leader may then change, too. Leadership implies followership. One person exerts influence or social power and others are influenced.

Group task roles. Members should help the group select and define common goals and work toward accomplishing them.

Suppose representatives of the school and community groups decide to work together to "do something about the drug problem." Members whose actions would be categorized in the task realm would "initiate" discussion of what could be done, or how the problem may be approached, or they may give new ideas for getting teenagers involved. Someone may offer "information" on what other groups in the city are doing and what official agencies are available for further help. Another may offer his "opinions" on the subject. Others may elaborate from their experience or reading.

With this variety of opinions and suggestions, some can "coordinate" or clarify the various suggestions in terms of which are appropriate for this group to work on and which are more appropriate for other groups. One person may summarize what has happened, perhaps point out deviations from the original goals, and raise questions as to whether the group can proceed as suggested or whether the group lacks the resources needed. (This person would be "orienting" the group.) There may be "critics" who question the facts or the effectiveness of the group. An "energizer" or "sensor" may prod the group and stimulate the members to greater creativity. There may be a "technician" who knows where materials on drugs may be obtained inexpensively; he may have access to a means of distributing leaflets or a speaker who could help clarify some of the technical questions. A "recorder" may be writing down suggestions, or making a record of group decisions on what has been assigned for the next meeting.

Group maintenance roles. While task roles focus on the problem-solving aspects of moving toward a goal, equally important, but at a different level, are the roles exhibited by the personal relations among group members.

At a meeting, members may sound as if they are giving information or opinions, or evaluating ideas. Frequently, the members may even attack one another on a personal level. A newcomer to the group may feel intimidated by this and be reluctant to present an idea. He may even reevaluate his status as to whether it is worthwhile to remain in the group. It is important for the "encouragers" and the "supporters" in the group to see that this does not happen. Other roles seen in the group maintenance situation are the "harmonizers" who attempt to mediate differences or relieve tension with a joke and the "gatekeepers" who notice whether or not everyone has had an opportunity to speak. These roles help a group maintain itself so that work on the task can proceed without interference.

Individual roles. Another set of roles is identified through members' individual needs. These needs are irrelevant to the group goals and are not conducive to helping the group work as a unit. An attack on one person leads to personal defense, joke telling may start "I can top that" jokes, and soon the goals of the group are forgotten as individuals attempt to satisfy individual needs.

In individual roles, we will find the "aggressor" giving a sarcastic opinion. The "blocker" saying the committee is useless unless they reach their goals, the "self-confessor" looking for sympathy, the "recognition-seeker" describing in glowing details how successful they have been, and the "dominator" attempting to take over by interrupting others, using flattery, or asserting a superior status. Of course, there are a few who may be "feelers" who base decisions on emotional highs and lows. A few may be "playboys" (or girls) who joke, keep bringing up unrelated subjects, or who have a conspicuous lack of interest in the real meeting. Are any of these people more or less valuable than the others? No! It is important to remember that each is valuable and can add to the direction of the group. Both task and maintenance roles are needed by the group.

Everyone who has ever led a committee has experienced the frustrations of trying to lead a group. We start off with a clear agenda, but time is always too short. How do you get the job done? First, recognize that there are two agendas:

1. Task—what is to be accomplished?
2. Needs—of the individual group members.

To accomplish anything, both these agendas must be met. Most groups think that they already know each other's needs and tasks. As a result, many groups plod on, mangle relationships, and blunder assignments.

Many groups operate using majority rule. Often, this results in the majority doing the project with a minority having far less enthusiasm for the task. It's better to develop a decision by consensus. This may force some to compromise, but the task will have "group ownership."
Then, develop good listening skills among group members. There are a lot of good ideas in groups that are never spoken because people feel no one is willing to really listen!
As a leader, periodically ask yourself these questions:

1. Does my group have a regular assigned meeting time?
2. Do we honor the commitment to meet?
3. Are people in the group made to feel worthwhile?
4. Do you practice consensus decision making?

5. Do you evaluate and hold each other accountable?
6. Does your small group treasure the times you are together?

If the answer to any of these questions is "no," your group is in trouble and needs to be reevaluated. If the answers were "yes," your group is probably okay. All you need is periodic fine-tuning.

The best groups are those whose members meet regularly, hold each other accountable, have a steady membership, feel ownership for assigned tasks, and care about each other.

MOTIVATING PEOPLE TO WORK ON GROUP TASKS

1. Make the members in your group want to do things (inspiration, incentive, recognition) and determine what makes each of them tick.
2. Be a good listener.
3. Criticize and approve constructively.
4. Criticize in private.
5. Praise in public.
6. Be considerate.
7. Delegate responsibility for details to members.
8. Give credit where it is due honestly.
9. Avoid domination or "forcefulness."
10. Show interest in and appreciation for the other person.
11. Make your wishes known by suggestions or request.
12. When you make a request or suggestion, be sure to explain the reasons for it.
13. Let the members in on your plans and programs, even when plans are at an early stage.
14. Never forget that the leader sets the style for members.
15. Play up the positive.
16. Be consistent.
17. Show members that you have confidence in them and that you expect them to do their best.
18. Ask members for their counsel and help.
19. When you are wrong or make a mistake, admit it.
20. Listen courteously to ideas from members.
21. If an idea is adopted or rejected, tell the originator why.
22. Give weight to the fact that people carry out their own ideas best.
23. Be careful of what you say and how you say it.
24. Don't be upset by little hassles.
25. Use every opportunity to build up in members a sense of the importance of their own work.
26. Share your goals, the sense of direction, something to strive for, and something to achieve.
27. Keep members informed on matters that affect them.
28. Give members a chance to take part in decisions, particularly those that affect them.

29. Let members know where they stand and why.
30. Make personal contact before and after meetings to encourage participation.
31. Give group members something to do immediately to keep interest levels high and to generate enthusiasm.
32. Use small groups and assign projects or put people on committees that interest them. This satisfies personal needs.
33. Remember that a met need is no longer a motivator. Continue to reassess members' needs and provide new challenges so that commitment to the task will be sustained.
34. Avoid assigning unnecessary tasks.
35. Encourage sharing without criticism or judgment.

FACILITATOR'S ROLE DURING TEAM BUILDING

YOUR ROLE DURING ACTIVITIES

The facilitator's role is to clearly present the situation, including safety procedures, and then to observe the group's efforts. You may occasionally need to remind the group of the situation as was originally presented. Instruct the group to make allowances for any physical handicaps. Be patient: Don't give hints or help.

YOUR ROLE AS OBSERVER

1. Notice your own "helper" feelings and remind yourself about whom you would be taking care of by giving hints. However, if the group becomes frustrated and defeated, you may want to encourage the group to search for a new approach. If the problem clearly will never be solved, you may give a hint. Sometimes it's better to stop and try the task at another time.
2. Make a few notes:
   a. Planning: Who suggested the first trial plan? Were the plans discussed? Was a method used for planning? How did the group handle failure? How did the final plan develop?
   b. Leadership styles: Which student leaders assumed they could do what was ruled out, e.g., "Why don't we just walk under it?" Did someone assume they couldn't do some things? e.g., "They said we couldn't pass the beam back and forth." Did the group act democratic, laissez-faire, or did a dictator arise? Were all members involved in the solution? Did one leader emerge? Was a leader appointed?
   c. Roles: What roles did people assume? Did they change roles? Who took positive roles? Who took negative roles? How did words and actions of group members cause others to act?
   d. Communication: How did the group communicate? What role did non-verbal communication play? Did aggressive members ignore quieter members? What were the strengths and weaknesses in communication?

YOUR ROLE DURING DEBRIEFING

During the debriefing, your role is that of facilitator. Allow the group members to discuss what happened to them individually and what they saw the group do. People will share a wide variety of feelings and perceptions about what happened. Ask the group about the same factors you were suggested to notice as an observer. Asking the right questions is the key to getting the students to process their experience. Share with the group points that you thought were important that the group members didn't notice. Trust your intuition.

TRANSFER

The most important aspect of processing the activity is helping members understand how the things they have learned about group dynamics relate to "real life." Ask them how the game relates to situations in the "real world" of your group, your meetings, school life, relationships, family, etc. For example, a student might observe:

"We all just tried to do the activity without first looking at the problem and formulating a plan. Sometimes in our group, we just start working and don't take time to think through what we should do."

WHENEVER I AM IN A GROUP SITUATION, I WILL....

Count My Blessings!

There is so much to learn from these people that I need to know (and only they can teach me). I will count what they have to offer as a blessing, and I will listen and learn.

Proclaim My Rarity!

I am the only me there is! Never in all the 70 billion humans who have walked this planet since the beginning of time has there been anyone exactly like me. Never, until the end of time, will there be another such as me.

I will proclaim my rarity by being the best me I can be. I cannot be someone else, only myself. I do not need to compete with other group members for each of us has our own gifts to give and all are valuable to the whole.

Therefore, I will be the best me I can be and encourage others to be their best selves.

Go the Extra Mile!

I know that nothing great was ever achieved without enthusiasm, and so I will tackle even the simplest of tasks with a positive attitude and gusto!

I will not expect others to praise me or reward me for going the extra mile: A job well done is its own reward. And I will not give 110% to outdo others or make them look less valuable. Cooperation, not competition, is the key to our group's success.

Whatever it is in my power to do, I will do with all my might!

Use Wisely My Power of Choice!

I will choose to belong rather than withdraw; cooperate rather than compete; create rather than destroy; encourage rather than tear down; listen rather than dominate; participate rather than abstain; praise rather than gossip; share rather than hoard!

I know that I can choose to be happy or sad, friendly or aloof, helpful or destructive, positive or negative. My choices will affect both the success of the group and the task we have been assigned. With so much at stake, I must choose wisely and I must be willing to take responsibility for the choices I make.

Whenever I am in a group situation, I will count my blessings, proclaim my rarity, go the extra mile, and use wisely my power of choice. And I will help to create a positive environment that allows the other members of the group to do the same.

By Earl Reum
Adapted from *Meetings That Matter* (1993).

GROUP PROCESS IDEAS

In general, a collection of people becomes a group when it possesses these qualities:

- A definable membership: a collection of two or more people identifiable by name or type or common interest.
- Group Consciousness: the members think of themselves as a group, have a "collective perception of unity."
- A shared sense of purpose (owned purpose).
- Interdependence in satisfaction of needs: the members need the help of one another to accomplish the purposes for which they joined the group. (A team is essential.)
- Interaction: The members communicate with each other, influence each other, react to one another.
- Ability to act as a unit.

Content vs. Process (The Gum vs. the Chewing)

It is important to note that there is a distinction between what a group is talking about and how the group is dealing with its communication. When we observe what the group is talking about, we are focusing on the content (gum). When we try to observe how the group is handling the content, i.e., who talks, how much, or who talks to whom, we are focusing on group process (chewing).

Most topics of group discussion emphasize the content: "What makes a good leader?" "What can we do to increase school spirit?" "How can we make meetings more effective?" and concern issues that are "there and then" and not involving the individual directly. In focusing on group process, we are looking at what the group is doing in the "here and now," how it is working in the sense of its present procedures and organization. Looking at process really means to focus on what is going on in the group and trying to understand it in terms of other things that have happened in the group.

Properties of Groups

In studying all types of groups, certain properties can be identified:

Background—Each group has a historical background, or lack of it, that influences its behavior. A new group coming together for the first time may have to devote much of its early energy to getting acquainted with one another and with the group's goals as well as establishing ways of working together. Members come into a meeting with some expectations about it. In some cases the boundaries around the group's freedom or action may be narrowly defined by the conditions under which it was created, or so poorly defined that the group doesn't know what its boundaries are.

Some questions that help to explain a group's background are:

- How well were members prepared to enter the group?
- What are their expectations about the group and their role in it?
- What is the composition of the group—what kind of people?
- What is their previous experience, prior friendship patterns?
- How were group members chosen?

- What arrangements have been made for this meeting—physical setting? Resources? Agenda? Support people?

Participation Patterns—Every group has a participation pattern. For instance, it may be all one-way, with the leader talking to the group members, or it may be two-way or multi-directional. In a given group this pattern may be consistent, or it may vary from time to time.

Some questions to ask which may reveal participation patterns are:

- Who talks? For how long? How often?
- Who do people look at when they talk?
- Do the members who don't talk much seem to be interested and listening?

It is sometimes useful to chart the participation pattern of groups during segments of a meeting. For example, pass a ball of yarn as each person participates and study the pattern formed.

Communication—This property has to do with how well group members understand one another—how clearly they are communicating their ideas, values, and feelings. If some members are using a highly specialized vocabulary, they may be talking over the heads of the rest of the group.

Do members frequently pick up contributions previously made and build on them with their own ideas? Do members feel free to ask for clarification when they don't understand a statement? Are responses to statements frequently irrelevant?

Cohesion—The cohesiveness of a group is identified by the bonds that bind the individual parts into a unified whole. This property indicates the morale, the team spirit, the strength of attraction of the group for its members, and the interest of the members in what the group is doing. Signs of weak cohesion include the emergence of cliques, factions, and such subgroupings as the "in group" or "their group."

Standards—Every group tends to develop a set of standards about what is acceptable behavior. Which subjects may be discussed, which are taboo, how openly members may express their feelings, the propriety of volunteering one's services, the length and frequency of statements considered allowable. A group might be confused about what its standards are and this may lead to embarrassment, irritation, and lost momentum.

What evidence is there that the group has a set of standards regarding such matters as self-discipline, sense of responsibility, tolerance of differences, freedom of expression, etc.?

Are there any marked deviations from these standards by one or more members of the group? With what effect?

Do these standards seem to be well-understood by all the members?

Which of the group's standards seem to help and which seem to hinder the group's progress?

Social Patterns—In every group the participants begin to identify certain individuals whom they like or agree with more than other members. These subtle relationships of friendship have an important influence on the group's activities. Some evidence indicates that people tend to agree more strongly and more often with people they like and to disagree more often with people they dislike, even though both express the same ideas.

Which members tend to identify with and support one another? Which members seem repeatedly in disagreement? Do some members act as "triggers" to others, causing them to respond immediately after the first member's comments, either pro or con?

Goals—All groups have goals: some long-range (i.e., "to promote the welfare of the school") or shorter-range objectives—("to plan a discussion on school spirit"). Some goals are clearly defined, specific, and publicly understood, and others may be vague, general, and only implicit. How does the group arrive at its goals? Are all members clear about them? Own them? Are all members committed to them? Are they realistic and attainable for the group?

SOME QUESTIONS ABOUT GROUP FUNCTIONING

Here are some questions that give students insight into group functioning:

Communication Patterns

1. Why was more than one person talking at one time?
2. Did I notice any patterns of response that may indicate that subgroups exist?
3. How do I feel about the seating arrangement? If I didn't like it, what could I do to change it?
4. Did the noise level of the group ever change? If so, why?
5. To whom are questions and comments usually addressed: the group, the leaders, or a particular member? Where is the power of the group?
6. Did I feel that I was communicating what I wanted to say?
7. Was the presentation style of others affecting my ability to listen?
8. What is getting in the way of effective group communication?

Content

1. Would it have helped for me to jot down important thoughts?
2. Did I stick to the topic?
3. Might I have found more value in listing several topics before discussing their merits (brainstorming) rather than getting bogged down on only one idea?
4. What ideas were presented to the group?
5. Were we too specific?
6. Did the group achieve a common understanding of the problem? The facts? The issues?
7. When others paraphrased my remarks, did they do it in a concise, accurate way? If not, why not? What could we do to improve this?
8. What was in the way of getting the content considered?

Decision Making

1. What blocked movement of the group?
2. What aided forward motion?
3. Was a definite decision made? Can I agree with it? Why?
4. Did I feel I contributed to the decision? Did I feel apart from it?
5. When the process became bogged down, would it have been helpful to take a break and/or start over?
6. Did the group test for general consensus?
7. What got in the way of effective decision making?

Leadership

1. What types of leadership did I perceive? How did I react to it?
2. What kinds of leadership roles did I fulfill?
3. What kinds of leadership did the group need? What did I do to help fill these needs?
4. Did I perceive any leadership struggles occurring?
5. What got in the way of effective leadership behavior?

Listening

1. Did I interrupt someone else? Was I continuously listening to other ideas or thinking of a response?
2. Did I clarify someone else's idea in my mind before offering an alternative?
3. Were the ideas expressed clearly? If not, what could I do to help clarify the ideas?
4. Do I have difficulty formulating thoughts and listening at the same time? What can I do about that?
5. What got in the way of effective listening during this meeting?

Maintenance

1. Did I disagree with anyone at any time? Could I have worded disagreement in a less threatening way?
2. How can I deal with another's needs? And how can I find out what other's needs are?
3. Here is a one-word description of the group (e.g., lackadaisical, cliquish, warm, cold, hostile, etc.):
4. Do members discard new ideas quickly? Do we explore one idea thoroughly before going on to the next?
5. What got in the way of group process being effective?

Non-Verbal Communication

1. Where did I look when I spoke?
2. How did I react to people's facial expressions?
3. What communication was happening while the verbal action was going on? Did anything get in the way of effectiveness?

Personal Performance

1. What things did I do in the group that I felt good about?
2. What things would I like to work on as an individual? What can I do to work on these issues?
3. Did I give verbal support to any ideas expressed?
4. What position in the group did I want to fill at a specific time? Are there others in the group

who were as capable as I to fill these positions? What other positions in the group did I not want to fill? Why?

5. When was I most uncomfortable in the group? Why?
6. Did I see myself in opposition to other members of the group? How can I work with them in a positive way?
7. What were my expectations about the group as I entered? As I left?
8. Did I feel free to ask for clarification when I didn't understand a statement?
9. What got in the way of effective personal performance for me?

Silence

1. Is a silent lapse of time necessarily bad in group discussion? What happens to my individual thinking during a silent period?
2. How do I deal with silence?
3. Did the more silent members seem interested in listening?
4. What are some non-threatening ways to bring a silent person into the discussion?
5. What nourished silence? What obstructed effective quiet reflection?

PROBLEMS IN GROUP RELATIONSHIPS

The solution to a problem is usually better if people work together on it. Successful group action in solving problems depends on several principles:

1. **Identification with other members.** Try to find out how the other person truly feels. (Do not assume that what you want is what others also want.) A discovery of common attitudes among members is a productive beginning.
2. **Participation.** Encourage everyone to take an active part. Consensus is much better than having an unhappy minority. People participate in individual ways and we must be tolerant and helpful in encouraging such participation.
3. **Democratic climate.** The job of the leader is to keep things moving and to let the group make decisions when they are ready to make them.
4. **Individual security.** People under tension often call names, get angry, exhibit prejudice, and behave in ways that destroy group cohesiveness. Security grows as trust develops within a group.
5. **Open lines of communication.** Explain and listen. Make the messages honest and accurate. Encourage the flow of listening, talking, responding.
6. **Improve listening.** We must attempt to interpret both the literal meaning and the intention of each speaker. We need to hear what "he" says, what "she" intends to say, and what "he" would have said if "he" could have said what "he" wanted to say. We must develop ways of checking our accuracy of hearing as well.
7. **Handling hostility.** Hostility in itself is not necessarily harmful to a group or even to individual productiveness. People need freedom to express hostility within a group because the inhibition of feelings decreases the efficiency of members. Controlled hostility can help the group move forward.

BASIC NEEDS OF PEOPLE IN GROUPS

Meetings involve people functioning as a group. As you consider the purposes for your meetings and create goals for them, consider the needs of the group members and how you will meet them. Here's what your group members are asking you to do:

Leader! If you want my loyalty, interest, and best efforts as a group member, you must take into account the fact that I need:

- A sense of belonging—to be a part of this family/group.
  A feeling that no one objects to my presence.
  A feeling that I am sincerely welcome and respected.
  A feeling that I am honestly needed for my total self, not just for my hands, my money, my connections.
  A feeling that I can work within this group and make a positive difference with my life.
- To have a share in planning the group goals. (My need will be satisfied only when I feel that my ideas have had a fair hearing.)
- To feel that the goals are within reach and that they make sense to me.
- To feel that what I'm doing contributes to human welfare—that its value extends beyond the group itself.
- To share in making the rules of the group—the rules by which we live and work toward our goals together.
- To know in some clear detail just what is expected of me so I can work confidently.
- To have responsibilities that challenge, that are within range of my abilities, and that contribute toward reaching our group goals.
- To see that progress is being made toward the goals we have chosen together.
- To be kept informed. (I will support you only when I know what's going on.)
- To have confidence in our leader—confidence based on consistent, fair treatment, recognition when it is due, trust, and loyalty.

In brief, this situation must make sense to me and I must feel success in being a part of it.

—Your member

7.3 GOAL SETTING

Meetings help organizations accomplish their goals, but to do that, they need objectives. The most common method of analyzing the goals you have established is the SMART goals method.

Am I being SMART about my goals?

S—Specific—What specifically do I intend to achieve?

M—Measurable—How will I know when I've achieved it? And to what degree?

A—Achievable—Is it realistic? Is it possible for me?

R—Responsible—Am I willing to be responsible for it? Am I able to be responsible for it? Is it controllable?

T—Timeframe—By when will I have accomplished it?

By Earl Reum

GOAL PLANNING

We can focus our students on the meeting itself by establishing goals. Use the following questions to help your group plan meetings.

What is our goal for the meeting? Specifically what do we intend to achieve? ____________________

____

What are the possible barriers to our success? ____________________

____

By when do we intend to achieve this? ____________________

What resources are available? ____________________

How will we measure our success? ____________________

____

Is this goal achievable, believable? ____________________

What are the immediate action steps? ____________________

____

Is this goal within our control? ____________________

____

How committed are we to achieving this goal? ____________________

____

____

____

7.4 SAMPLE MEETING SCRIPT FOR OFFICERS

This sample meeting script will give inexperienced officers an idea of the flow of a meeting and help build their confidence before that all-important first meeting. Consider reading through this script at the meeting where your meeting agenda is planned.

Prior to the meeting:

- Meet with the Executive Committee to plan and review the meeting agenda.
- Distribute a copy of the agenda to all members or make it available for viewing.
- Identify a presiding officer for the meeting and take time with this individual to review the agenda items.
- Notify individuals with specific responsibilities at the upcoming meeting (e.g., secretary, treasurer, committee chairs, project chairs, etc.) indicating the nature of their duties for the meeting and when they appear on the agenda.
- Notify members and remind them of the meeting time and place. Note: Sometimes more than one notification is required.
- Secure the room/location for the meeting and see that all supplies for attendees are available, including the gavel for the presiding officer and an American flag if the Pledge of Allegiance is to be included in the meeting.

I. CALL TO ORDER:

President (or other presiding officer): "The September 20th meeting of the South Lakes Chapter of the National Honor Society is now called to order." (Rap gavel twice.)
Pledge of Allegiance: "Please stand and recite with me the Pledge of Allegiance." (Face the flag, "I pledge allegiance to the flag....")
President: "Thank you. You may be seated."

II. ROLL CALL:

President: "I now call upon the Chapter Secretary, (identify the secretary by name), to take the roll."
Secretary: Following the completion of the roll call (whether orally or an alternative method), the Secretary announces whether quorum* has been reached for the meeting.
Secretary: "Mr./Ms. President, there are ___ members present and a quorum has/has not been established."
President: "Thank you."

III. MINUTES:

President: "Will the secretary now please read the minutes of the last meeting?"
Secretary: Reads the minutes. Note: Minutes should be written, reviewed, and approved by the president and adviser prior to presentation at this meeting to minimize the need for corrections, additions, deletions, etc.
President: "Are there any additions or corrections to the minutes?" (Members provide corrections if there are any.) "If there are no (further) corrections or additions to the minutes, I will ask for a motion to approve the minutes as read (corrected)."
Chapter member: "I move to approve the minutes as read (corrected)."
Another member: "I second the motion." (There is no discussion on this motion.)

President: "All those in favor, say 'aye'." [Group votes]
"All those opposed, say 'nay'." [Group votes.]
President: Announce if the motion passed or not. "The motion passes/does not pass."

IV. TREASURER'S REPORT:

President: "Will the Treasurer, identify by name, now please give the treasurer's report?"
Treasurer: Presents report. At the conclusion: "Mr./Ms. President, I present this report for your approval."
President: "Thank you. Are there any questions?" Field questions that arise; allow treasurer to provide explanations as needed. At the conclusion of the discussion:
President: "Without any (further) questions or objections, the report is approved as presented." (Rap gavel once.)

V. COMMITTEE REPORTS:

President: "We will now ask for Committee Reports." Using a master list of current committees, the president can ask each chairperson if he or she has a report to make. Allow the reports to be given. Thank each report giver upon the completion of his or her report and ask the group if there are any questions for that committee. Note: Committee chairs should be given a time limit for their reports (e.g., two minutes) prior to the meeting. Written summaries or handouts can facilitate the expeditious handling of committee reports.

VI. OLD/UNFINISHED BUSINESS:

President: "We will now move on to unfinished business. The first item of unfinished business is....." Review each item of Unfinished Business in the order provided on the meeting Agenda.
President: "Are there any other items of New Business for today? If not, we will now move on to New Business."

VII. NEW BUSINESS:

President: "We will begin the New Business with the consideration of...." Review New Business items from the Agenda.
President: "Are there any additional items of New Business? (pause) If not, we will now have additional Reports and Announcements."

VIII. REPORTS AND ANNOUNCEMENTS:

[Sections VIII and IX can be switched per preferences.]
President: "Are there any reports or announcements for the group?"
Many chapters will begin reports/announcements with input from the chapter adviser. The president recognizes each report/announcement giver by name (and title where relevant); ask presenters to stand. Upon completion, thank each presenter and ask if there are any additional reports or announcements.

IX. PROGRAM:

President: "We will now move to the program for today's meeting." Introduces the program speaker or other activity or event for the meeting.
Presentation (with a pre-set time limit).
At the conclusion of the presentation, thank the presenter by name and offer a reference to the value of the content to the group.

X. ADJOURNMENT:

President: "Thanks to everyone for attending today's meeting. A final reminder that our next regularly scheduled meeting is set for Tuesday, October 16. If there is no further business (pause), I will ask for a motion to adjourn the meeting."
Member: "I move to adjourn the meeting."
Another member: "I second the motion." This is non-debatable; proceed to the vote.
President: (If approved) "The September meeting of the South Lakes NHS chapter is now adjourned." (Rap gavel once.)

Note: If the chapter wishes to adjourn the meeting before all the business has been completed, the meeting must be adjourned by a motion.

*Quorum: Standard quorum rules call for at least 50% of members to be present to conduct official business. A different quorum level can be developed and included in the group's bylaws. Failure to have a quorum simply means that no official business can be conducted, though reports and program components can be presented.

7.5 SECRETARY'S WORKSHEET

Meeting of____

Date______________ Time________________ Place________________

Presiding Officer ____

Members Present ____

Absent ____

Minutes of Previous Meeting____

(State if accepted, corrected, etc)

Officer's Reports ____

Treasurer's Report ____

Committee Reports (and actions taken as a result of these reports)

1. Report of committee on____

   Presented by______________written report__________ (attached)verbal __________

   Recommendations or motion ____

   Maker of motion______________ seconded by____________ Vote: for____ against _____

2. Report of committee on ____

   Presented by______________written report__________ (attached)verbal __________

   Recommendations or motion ____

   Maker of motion______________ seconded by____________ Vote: for____ against _____

Business (Carried Over) (Unfinished Business)

   Item______________________________ Presented by______________

   Action ____

   Maker of motion______________ seconded by____________ Vote: for____ against _____

New Business (for each item record action taken, if referred to committee. List it if action is taken; record it. If it is deferred, list it for next time.)

1. Item______________________________ Presented by ______________

   How handled? ____

2. Item______________________________ Presented by______________

   How handled? ____

Announcements or Other Reports (those requiring no action—attach copies to minutes)

1. reported by____
2. reported by____
3. reported by____

New Committees Appointed (include task assigned)

1. ____

   Members ____

   Task assigned______________________________ Date report due______________

2. ____

   Members ____

   Task assigned______________________________ Date report due______________

Summary of Program____

Guest Present ____

Adjournment____

(Time of adjournment and how)

Signature of Secretary: ____

Note: Collect a copy of all reports given and attach them to the minutes. Check with absentees. Type up a summary for members, adviser, and administration.

7.6 ACTIVITY PLANNING GUIDES

Planning any activity requires careful thought and preparation. Before stepping into action, be sure that you can answer the following questions:

1. What are you planning to do?

2. Why do you want to do this project?

3. When and where will the activity take place?

4. Who will benefit from the project?

5. Which staff members will need to approve the project?

6. What funds are needed?

7. When will the basic planning be done?

8. What committees are necessary?

9. What kind of publicity is needed?

10. Who deserves a special thank you?

11. Was the project worthwhile?

12. What's next? Where do we go from here?

ACTIVITY PLANNING SHEET

Today's Date:

Type of Activity: ________________________________

Sponsor: ________________________________

Name or theme of event: ________________________________

Name of person in charge: ________________ Home phone: ________________

Date of event: ________________ Time: ________________

Location of event: ________________________________

Who is the event for? ________________________________

Budgeted amount for publicity: ________________________________

Methods of publicity: ________________________________

Frequency of event: ❑ daily ❑ weekly ❑ biweekly ❑ monthly ❑ quarterly ❑ annually

Will tickets be needed? ________________ When? ________________

Ticket price: ________________

Ticket outlet locations: ________________

When? ________________

Ticket sale deadline: ________________

Seating arrangements: ________________________________

Parking arrangements: ________________________________

Dress: ________________________________

Refreshments: ________________________________

When should publicity begin? ________________________________

Kinds of publicity: ________________________________

❑ Newspaper ❑ Radio ❑ TV ❑ Magazine ❑ Flyers ❑ Banners ❑ Billboards

Other: ________________________________

Printed programs: ___Yes ___No When? ________________________________

Who is doing this? ________________________________

Information for the program: ________________________________

____

Special theme/logo/colors that should be used with publicity: ________________

____

Information about performing group, special guests, or speakers: ________________

News Elements: ________________________________

Additional information, ideas, or suggestions: ________________________________

____

Report Submitted By: ________________________________

To: ________________________________

7.7 MEETINGS TO SOLVE PROBLEMS: A WORKSHEET

1. What is the nature of the problem?
2. Should it be approached through a meeting?
3. Are many involved?
4. Can personalities be kept out?
5. Will the group be open-minded?
6. Should everyone get the same story?
7. Will a meeting save time?
8. What do you want to accomplish as a result of the meeting?
9. What type of meeting should it be? (Check one, based on the purpose of meeting.)
   - ❑ Informational—to pass on some information the group members do not have.
   - ❑ Directed Discussion—to get them to understand and accept an established decision.
   - ❑ Explorational—to obtain facts, ideas, or opinions from the group.
   - ❑ Problem Solving—to get the group to make the decisions necessary to solve the problem.
10. Who should attend the meeting?
11. Would it be helpful to give members time to think about the problem before the meeting?
12. What should be the title of the meeting?
13. What objectives should be given to the group?
14. What parts of the problem need to be discussed by the group to accomplish the objectives of the meeting?
15. How will you draw out or present facts, ideas, or opinions related to these activities?
16. How will you get the group to evaluate the facts, ideas, or opinions to get acceptance of an established decision?
17. Who needs to learn the results of the meeting?
18. Next steps? Other considerations?

7.8 MEETING MANAGEMENT RESOURCES

Looking for some good resources to help you lead effective meetings? First, consider purchasing a copy of *Parliamentary Procedure Without Stress* by Roberta M. McDow, available, along with other helpful publications for student activities groups, from NASSP.

You will also find a wealth of information on the Internet. (Note: These references are for general information purposes only; their listing here does not constitute an official endorsement by NHS, NJHS, NASC, or NASSP):

Effective Meetings

This business consultant's Web site has a variety of tools, including a helpful article on how to have effective meetings.

www.toolpack.com/meetings.html

How to Lead Effective Meetings

The Office of Human Resource Development at the University of Wisconsin-Madison has put together an extensive section of streaming audio files and articles on how to lead effective meetings.

www.ohrd.wisc.edu/academicleadershipsupport/howto1.htm

Key to Effective Meetings Game

This game provides an opportunity for students to practice what they've learned about the functions, requirements, and characteristics of effective meetings by role-playing as participants in a meeting.

http://edweb.sdsu.edu/courses/EDTEC670/Cardboard/board/e/effectivemeetings/keymeetings.html

Meeting Resource Center

Whether you're a newcomer to meetings or a seasoned pro, this resource center offers hands-on meeting advice for every possible situation.

www.effectivemeetings.com/

Snap Meetings

This site, run by the American Institute of Parliamentarians, offers a 10-lesson online correspondence course designed for the beginning presiding officer or board member who wants to know the basics of parliamentary procedure. The course uses Robert's Rules of Order Newly Revised, 10th Edition, includes .PDF study materials for each topic, and requires successful completion of an online exam to receive the final completion certificate.

www.snapmeetings.com

Taking Minutes

Robert McConnell Productions offers *McMinutes: A Training Manual for Secretaries*, which features a video and training manual the duties of a Secretary and how to perform these duties.

www.parli.com

National Association of Parliamentarians (NAP)

This Web site of the National Association of Parliamentarians has a variety of basic how-to information that is very helpful.

www.parliamentarians.org/procedure.php

Parliamentary Procedure

This wonderful site sponsored by Jim Slaughter, parliamentarian, attorney, and parliamentary procedure consultant has a wealth of free articles on aspects of parliamentary procedure, including a "cheat sheet" that outlines what to say in various situations—such as when you want to close debate or register a complaint—as well as a parliamentary strategy article, a matching quiz on parliamentary motions, and much more.

www.jimslaughter.com

American Institute of Parliamentarians (AIP)

The official site of the American Institute of Parliamentarians includes book links and information on becoming a certified parliamentarian.

www.parliamentaryprocedure.org/

Parliamentary Procedure Online

This site features some general information including some quizzes, an online tutorial, and mind benders to keep your meetings in order.

www.parlipro.org

Robert's Rules of Order

The official site of *Robert's Rules of Order* features information about the authors who have created the leading manual of parliamentary procedure, how you can use Robert's Rules of Order Newly Revised to help your organization run more smoothly, and how to order the current edition.

www.robertsrules.com/

Robert's Rules Online

This site offers the full text of the original fourth edition of *Robert's Rules of Order Revised* (which is not the current edition), including lesson outlines and Plan for Study of Parliamentary Law, along with the added convenience and functionality of index and keyword search.

www.rulesonline.com

We hope you find this information helpful as you pursue the effective management of your meetings. Is there a motion to adjourn?

7.9 STATEMENT OF THE NATIONAL ASSOCIATION OF SECONDARY SCHOOL PRINCIPALS ON STUDENT ACTIVITIES

Issue:

Beyond the standard curriculum of required and elective courses, schools enhance student learning and development by offering a range of cocurricular student activities. Activities can be classified into four distinct categories:

- Direct extensions of required or elective courses (e.g., science club, math club, dance club, etc.), including opportunities for recognition of achievements in those areas through honorary organizations (e.g., National Honor Society, Quill and Scroll, Spanish Honor Society, Tri-M Honor Society, etc.).
- Clubs or activities that are expressions of student interest that may be interdisciplinary in nature or not have a direct curricular link (e.g., popular music club, skateboarding club, etc.).
- Student council or student government that serve as opportunities for students to engage in the democratic process and have a voice in the life of the school to the extent allowable by law, policy, or tradition.
- Interscholastic and intramural athletics that provide students opportunities for development through sport (e.g., football, track, tennis, cheerleading, etc.).

NASSP Guiding Principles:

- Secondary schools properly provide for social and personal needs, as well as for those that are strictly academic. Student activities are integral to an education, providing opportunities for all students that support and extend academic learning.
- The term "student activities" is preferred to "extracurricular" since "extra" connotes activities that are peripheral to a school's main mission. Student activities are educational in nature and should be thought of as cocurricular.
- Student Activities support the goal of teaching students to be responsible and fulfilled human beings, providing them with opportunities that develop character, critical thinking, sociability, and specific skills.
- Research has shown a strong relationship between participation in student activities and academic achievement.
- Membership in national and state student activities organizations adds value to programs sponsored at the local level by providing training and other services, unique opportunities for networking, and additional recognition for those involved.

Recommendations:

- Recognize all activities carried out under the aegis of a secondary school in terms of their potential contribution to the school's overall goals for young people.
- Encourage secondary schools to engage as many students as possible in student activities and offer sufficient variety to appeal to a wide range of student interests.
- Encourage administrators, educators, student activity advisers and the general public to use the term "student activities" instead of "extracurricular activities." Student handbooks, school documents, and other communication should reflect this more current terminology.

- Ensure that activities are age-appropriate; non-discriminatory; well planned, organized, and implemented; supervised by professional staff; and evaluated on a regular basis.
- Ensure that participation in events sponsored by state and national organizations for youth be subject to identifiable minimum standards for the quality of the program, its content, and its practices regarding participant supervision and safety.
- Ensure that staff directing student activities receive professional development in the area of responsibility, and appropriate compensation for the work provided while fulfilling this supervisory duty.

Approved by the NASSP Board of Directors
November 9, 2002

BOOK EVALUATION FORM

We know how important evaluation is to improving your product or process. Please share with us some of your reactions to this book by completing the brief questionnaire below.

1. Overall evaluation (check one): How would you rate the value of this publication to your work in student activities?
   __ Excellent
   __ Good
   __ Adequate
   __ Poor. Here's why: ____

2. What is one thing that you like most about this publication? ____________________

3. For upcoming publications, would you prefer to receive such texts on a CD or simply posted for downloading as PDF documents on a Web site? I would prefer:
   ___ CD version
   ___ Web site download
   ___ Printed editions
   Other concepts/thoughts to share on this concept of making publications available to members? ____

4. What else would you like to see in this publication that isn't currently here? (Additional topics, other resources, etc.) ____

Do you have any additional comments or suggestions for the authors on any topic related to student activities and advising?____

Please help us learn a little more about you.
Name (optional): ____________________________
Years served as activity adviser?____________________________
State (Please include): ____________________________

Mail or fax this evaluation to:
Meetings That Matter Evaluation
c/o NASSP Student Activities Office
1904 Association Drive
Reston, VA 20191
Fax: 703-476-5432
E-mail: nhs@nhs.us

Thanks for taking the time to evaluate this new publication! Your comments are appreciated.

ORDERING INFORMATION

Meetings That Matter, Revised Edition (2007)
Product Number: 6200701

To order additional copies, please contact NASSP sales toll free at 866-647-7253, Monday through Friday, 8:30 a.m.–4:30 p.m. EST or visit our stores online at www.nhs.us/store, www.njhs.us/store, or www.nasc.us/store to order additional copies. Quantity discounts are available.

NOTES

NOTES

NOTES

NOTES